rasIsland

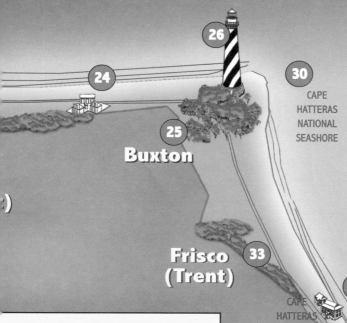

24

26

30

CAPE
HATTERAS
NATIONAL
SEASHORE

25

Buxton

**Frisco
(Trent)**

33

36

CAPE
HATTERAS
NATIONAL
SEASHORE

37

40

**Hatteras
Village**

Hatteras
Ferry
Landing

To
Ocracoke
Island

Tour Sites

nnakeet Life-Saving Station
et/Avon
lover

atteras Lighthouse
int
ent)
Hill Coast Guard Station
let Site
Village

g tour sites.)

Rodanth[e]

A T[

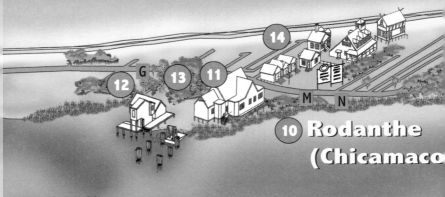

G · 13 · 11 · 12 · 14

M N

10 Rodanthe
(Chicamaco[

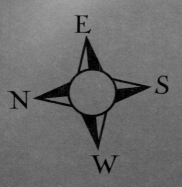

E

N   S

W

Index of Spor[

Island Gift Shop -----
Hatteras Island Wate[
Hotline Thrift Shop -
Camp Hatteras ------
Down Under Restaur[
Leonardo's Restaura[
Midgett Realty ------
Ocean Annies -------
Hatteras Island Surf
Outer Beaches Realt[
St. Waves Plaza -----
Fishin' Hole ---------
Sun Realty -----------
Surf or Sound Realty

Recreation   Re[

he/Waves

LANTIC O

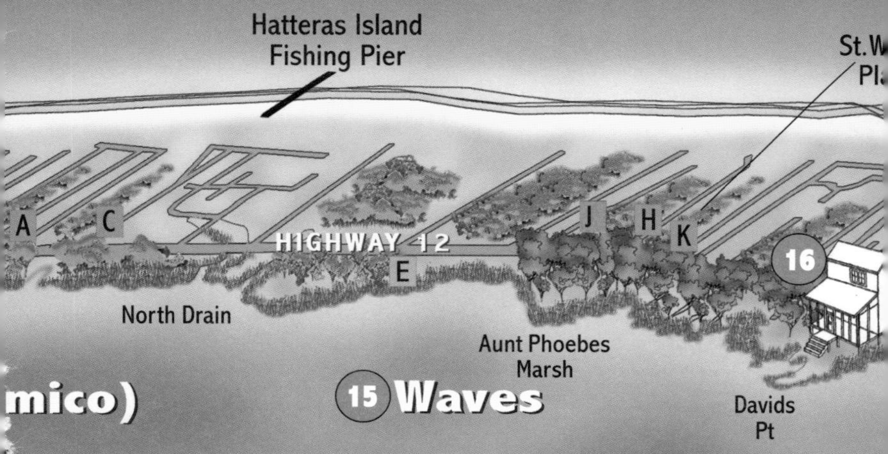
Hatteras Island
Fishing Pier
St.W
Pl
A
C
J
H
K
HIGHWAY 12
E
16
North Drain
Aunt Phoebes
Marsh
mico)
15 Waves
Davids
Pt

sors Located in Rodanthe, Waves and Salvo

	A	Page 117
rsports	B	Page 111
	C	Page 116
	D	Page 167
ant	E	Page 141
nts	F	Page 143
	G	Inside Front Cover
	H	Page 118
& Sail	I	Page 111
	J	Inside Back Cover
	K	Page 117
	L	Page 119
	M	Page 172
	N	Page 172A

staurant Shopping Accommodation

P

10 Rodar
11 Rodar
12 Rodar
13 Live (
14 Chica

Hatter

HIGHWAY 12

CAPE HATTERAS NATIONAL SEASHORE

19

20
Avon
(Kinnakeet

17 Salvo

Waves
he
mico)

Hatteras Island Area Driving

(Please refer to the individual area maps for more drivi

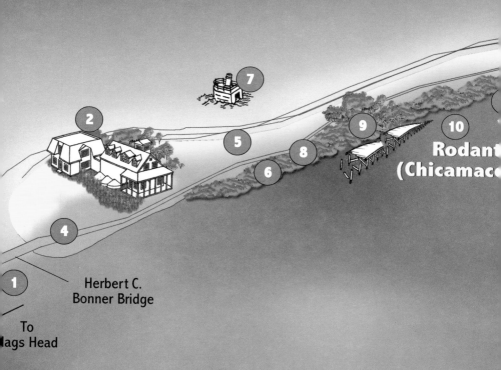

ATLANTIC
OCEAN

PAMLICO
SOUND

Herbert C.
Bonner Bridge

To
Nags Head

Rodant
(Chicamace

E
S
N
W

/Salvo

CEAN

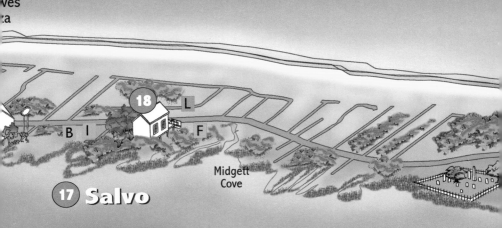

ves
.a

18

L

B I

F

Midgett
Cove

17 **Salvo**

AMLICO SOUND

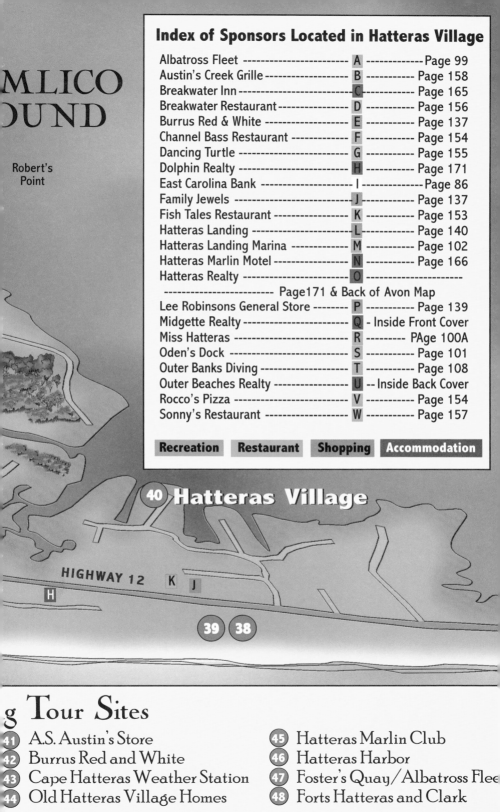

MLICO OUND

Robert's Point

Index of Sponsors Located in Hatteras Village

Recreation **Restaurant** **Shopping** **Accommodation**

40 Hatteras Village

HIGHWAY 12   K J

H

39 38

g Tour Sites

41 A.S. Austin's Store
42 Burrus Red and White
43 Cape Hatteras Weather Station
44 Old Hatteras Village Homes

45 Hatteras Marlin Club
46 Hatteras Harbor
47 Foster's Quay/Albatross Flee
48 Forts Hatteras and Clark

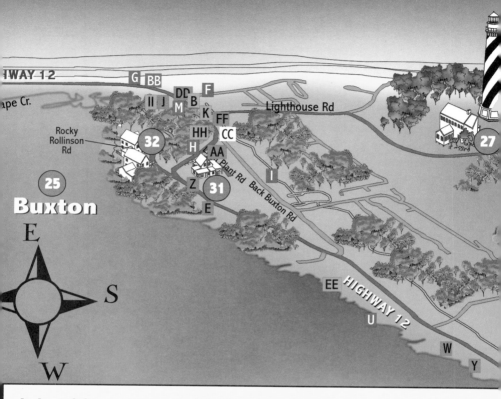

ATLANTIC

HWAY 12
ape Cr.

G BB

II J DD
M B F
K

Rocky
Rollinson
Rd

32

25

Buxton

Lighthouse Rd

FF
HH CC
H AA
Plant Rd Back Buxton Rd
Z 31
E

I

27

EE HIGHWAY 12
U

W

Y

E

S

W

Index of Sponsors Located in Buxton & Frisco

Recreation **Restaurant** **Shopping** **Accommodation**

PA
S

MV Australia Way

Kohler Rd

45

Saxon
Cut

43

44

41

Kohler Rd

E

I

42

The Slash

F

U

T

V

O

Drivin

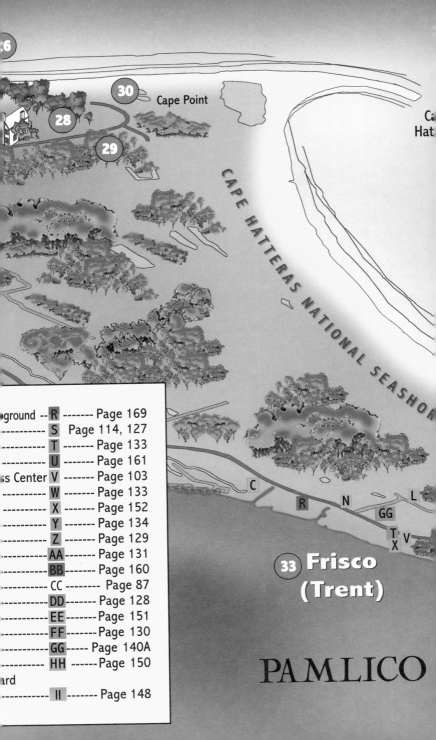

OCEAN

26

30 Cape Point

28

29

CAPE HATTERAS NATIONAL SEASHOR

Ca
Hat

C

R   N   GG   L

T
X   V

33 Frisco
(Trent)

PAMLICO

Hatteras
Village

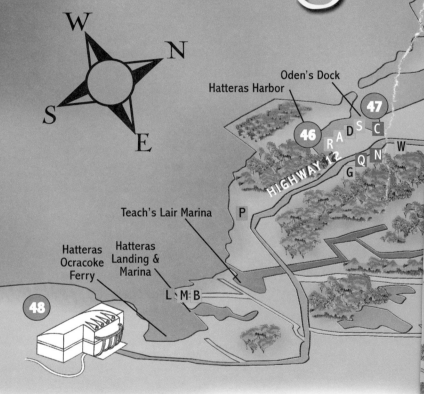

W N
S E

Oden's Dock

Hatteras Harbor

47

46

R A D S C

12

HIGHWAY 12

Q N

G

W

Teach's Lair Marina

P

Hatteras
Ocracoke
Ferry

Hatteras
Landing &
Marina

48

L M B

ATLANTIC
OCEAN

Buxton
&Frisco

Driving Tour Sites

25 Buxton
26 Cape Hatteras Lighthouse
27 Double Keepers' Quarters and Principal Keeper's Quarters
28 Former CCC Camp
29 Graves of British Seamen
30 Cape Point
31 The Old Gray House
32 Rocky Rollinson Road
33 Frisco/Trent
34 Old Trent Area
35 Frisco Native American Museum
36 Creed's Hill Coats Guard Station

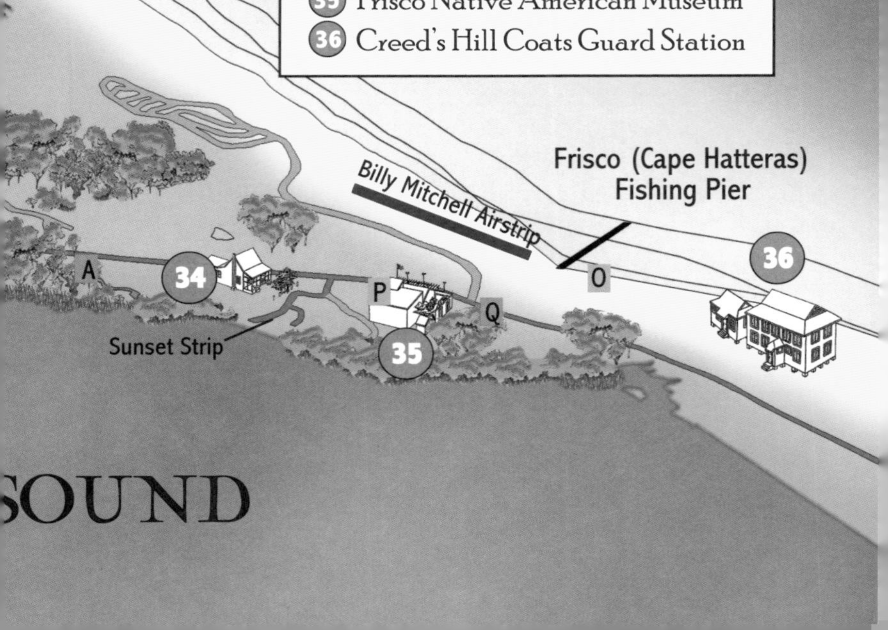

Billy Mitchell Airstrip

Frisco (Cape Hatteras) Fishing Pier

A

34

Sunset Strip

P

35

Q

O

36

SOUND

E
S
N
W

A T L A

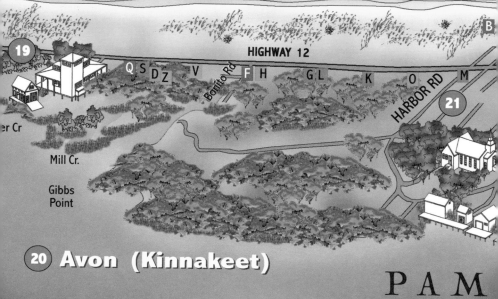

19

HIGHWAY 12

Q S D Z V | F H G L K O M

Bonito Rd

HARBOR RD

21

er Cr

Mill Cr.

Gibbs
Point

20 **Avon (Kinnakeet)**

P A M

dex of Sponsors Located in Avon

creation   Restaurant   Shopping   Accommodation

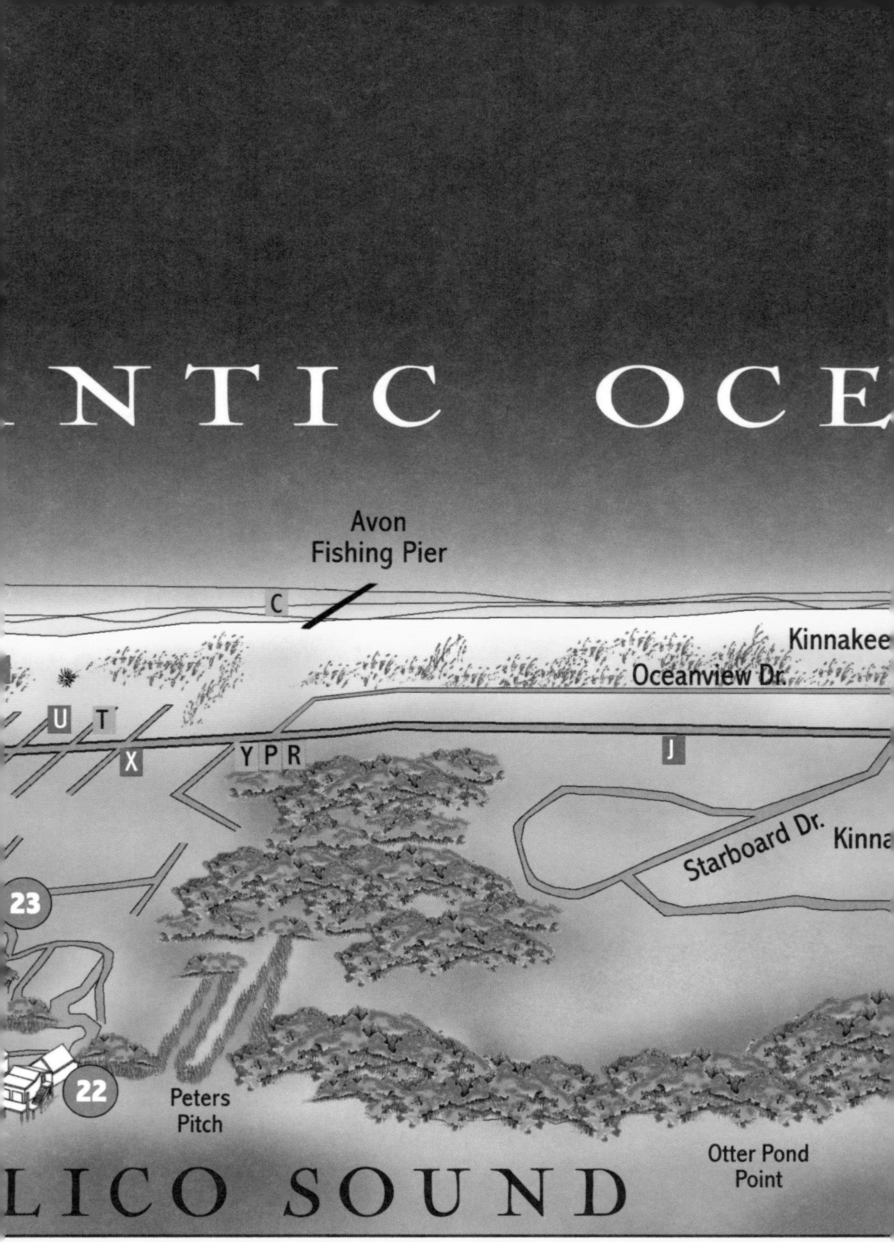
NTIC OCE
Avon
Fishing Pier
C
Kinnakee
Oceanview Dr.
U
T
X
Y P R
J
Starboard Dr.
Kinna
23
22
Peters
Pitch
Otter Pond
Point
LICO SOUND

ck of This Map			
Page 123	Ninos Pizza	R	Page 143
Page 122	Ocean Annie's	S	Page 120
Page124	Ocean Atlantic Rentals	T	Page 113
Page 84A	Outer Beaches Realty	U	Inside Back Cover
Page 132B	Sailworld	V	Page 113
Page 125	Sun Realty	W	Page 172
Inside Front Cover	Surf or Sound Ltd	X	Page 172A
	Village Video	Y	Page 107
	Windsurfing Hatteras	Z	Page 112

over the Outer

acation You've Be

Hatteras Realty, we're more than just a
e're a complete resort community. Ever
acation includes exclusive amenities the
nywhere else. Enjoy miles of pristine wh
eautiful Hatteras Island, and EVERY hom
our *Club Hatteras* resort amenities FREE!

Choose from over 470 Beach Vac
Club Hatteras Resort Amenities Designed F

- Huge Heated Pool with
  Sundeck and Chaises
- 6-Hole Putting Green
- Concession Stand
- Cabana with
  Bathrooms & Showers

- 2 Re
  Ten
- Kids
  & Pi

m for our complete online rental brochure
s, or call 800-HATTERAs. (800-428-8372) to r

Avon

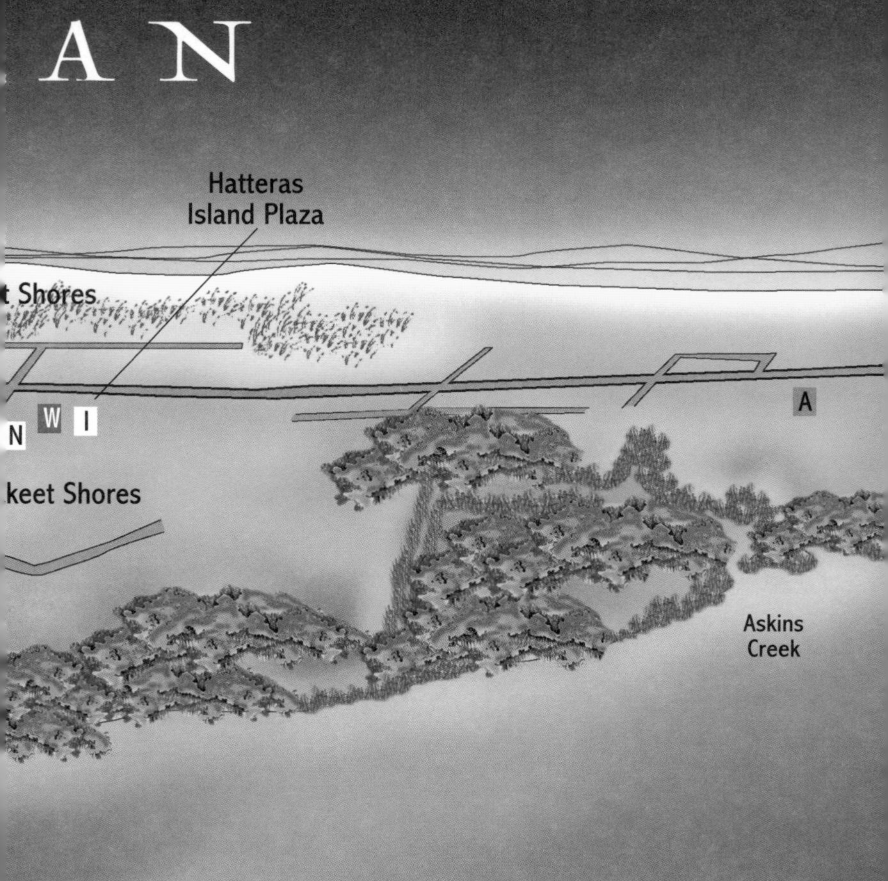

AN

Hatteras
Island Plaza

t Shores

N W I

keet Shores

A

Askins
Creek

Driving Tour Sites

19. Little Kinnakee Life-Saving Station
20. Kinnakeet / Avon
21. Old Kinnakeet Area
22. Avon Harbor
23. St John United Methodist Church

Disc
V.

At
we
vc
a
b
d

Hatter
Real

One Boat Guides

Hatteras
Island
Driving Tour & Guidebook

SECOND EDITION

Hatteras Island
Driving Tour & Guidebook

by Molly Harrison

Published by Narayana, Inc.
DBA One Boat Guides
Michael McOwen, Publisher
P.O. Box 308 • Manteo, NC 27954

(252) 202-5548
e-mail: MMMcOwen@earthlink.net

2nd Edition
2nd Printing

Printed in the United States of America

ISBN 0-9768164-0-7

SAN: 256-517X

About the cover:

On Friday morning, April 29th 1955, the first Pirate's Jamboree was held at the Cape Hatteras Lighthouse. The Coastland Times reported that ". . . a fish fry will be served near the lighthouse at Buxton. Nearby will be the beauty contest and also the pony and buggy races."

The black and white photo was slightly modified and color was added through computer enhancement by the publisher.

Table of Contents ❧

Photo Courtesy: Outer Banks History Center

Acknowledgments

Working on this book was both joyful and frustrating; joyful because of the chance to meet so many interesting people and learn so much about Hatteras Island, frustrating because there is so much rich history about Hatteras that there was no way to include it all in this book. Many things I heard and learned just don't have a home here and I hate to see them not being shared.

So many people on Hatteras Island were eager and willing to help, to share a story or to pass along a lead or to set me straight on the facts. I owe a great deal of gratitude to Danny Couch, whose love of Hatteras Island history is contagious. I was the only person on one of Danny's first bus tours of the island, and he generously shared his knowledge with me. If you want to hear more stories that couldn't be included here, Danny's Hatteras Island Tours are the way to go.

Others who generously gave me their time and memories were Dale Burrus, Ernie and Lynne Foster, Grace Peele, Salina Farrow, Mildred Poole, Natalie Perry, Manson Meekins, Gloria O'Neal, Erlene Willis, Carol Dillon, Eddie Skakel, Dan Oden, Dewey Parr, Edward Hooper and Carl Bornfriend, but there were many others all over the island who passed along valuable tidbits and priceless information.

Everybody at the Outer Banks History Center was extremely helpful — Sarah, Kelly, Kaeli and Lois; thanks for always being there to help with research. Thanks also to Steve Harrison of the National Park Service for his diligent research on the Outer Banks Life-Saving Stations and his generosity in donating his work to the History Center.

Thanks also to all the authors whose work gave this book fodder and helped me put things into perspective: David Stick's *The Outer Banks of North Carolina*, *An Outer Banks Reader* and *The Graveyard of the Atlantic*; Ben Dixon MacNeill's *The Hatterasman*; Dawson Carr's *The Cape Hatteras Lighthouse*; Jay Barnes's *North Carolina's Hurricane History* and many others. Also helpful were back issues of *The Island Breeze* and *The Sea Chest*, an incredible publication of island memories put out by the Cape Hatteras High School students in decades past.

Another great resource was the Hatteras Village Guided Tour, a publication of the Hatteras Village Civic Association. This and the historical survey of Nancy Van Dolsen were very helpful, and the people responsible for documenting the Hatteras Village history should be proud.

A great thank you to all the Hatteras business owners, who made the job of compiling the guidebook section easier with their willingness to help.

Thanks to Buddy Swain and Hatteras Designs, Inc for use of the Isabel photos.

Gary Crane deserves credit and kudos for the illustrations on the maps, and Elaine Danis is gratefully appreciated for her work on the maps, advertising, guidebook section and the website. Thanks to Beth Storie for her editorial expertise, and to Publisher Michael McOwen for thinking of me to work on such a fun project. **MH**

Introduction ❧

What is it about an island that is so intriguing, so special, so alluring? Why is it that an island is so altogether different from the mainland? That the mere mention of the word makes our faces soften and our breath slow down? Why does a piece of land surrounded by water call out to us, creating an intense longing to visit its banks and shores?

Photo Courtesy: Outer Banks History Center

purify stale lungs, and warm sand to soften hardened soles. The island calls out to the adventurer in all of us, enticing us with tales of surfing a storm-induced swell, riding the wind with a kite and a board, and battling a blue marlin the size of a small bus. Hatteras calls to the naturalist in all of us, luring us in to see brown pelicans belly-skimming the ocean surface, sea turtle tracks etched into the beach, and dolphins arcing their pointed fins in the sea.

Hatteras is like any other island in this respect. Its Atlantic Ocean beaches, Pamlico Sound marshes and undeveloped sandscapes call to the weary soul in all of us, promising breath-taking sunrises as a respite for strained eyes, healing salt air to

Hatteras Island is the perfect combination of natural world and vacation world. More than 60 percent of the island is in its almost-natural barrier island state,

thanks to the protection of the Cape Hatteras National Seashore and Pea Island National Wildlife Refuge. More than half of the island is open land or cultural sites waiting to be explored. The rest of the island caters to visitors with hotels and motels, rental homes from the luxurious to the simple, restaurants from family style to upscale contemporary, locally owned shops offering just about everything you could need and recreation opportunities for everyone.

Thanks to bridges and a well-run ferry system, Hatteras Island is not as remote as it once was. But still, the island is out-of-the-way enough to make going there feel like a veritable getaway. Even northern Outer Bankers, who live less than an hour away, like to escape to Hatteras Island. This is because, for the most part, Hatteras Island has been able to retain its own unique culture and attitude. For its residents and visitors, Hatteras offers a simple lifestyle in tune with nature and connected to the roots of its history. So far, superstores and chain restaurants and cookie-cutter consumerism haven't crossed the waters that surround Hatteras Island. This is not to say that the modern world isn't slowly seeping in. This is best exemplified in a bumper sticker seen around the island: "Slow down, this ain't the mainland." This may be a reference to driving habits, but it applies to much more.

If Hatteras Island is intriguing for what it offers today, it is even more so because of its past. Hatteras's history speaks of the sea, of lighthouses, shipwrecks on the island's infamous shoals, the lifesaving efforts of courageous locals and the island's vulnerability in times of war. It speaks of islanders living in what sounds like an idyllic setting with gardens and livestock and the bounty of the sea, but what was really a struggle in the face of hurricanes and the hardships of isolation. The stories of Hatteras's past are so rich and colorful that it's a shame no single book will ever be able to contain them.

If you're hearing the call of Hatteras Island, this book is for you. The first part of the book guides you along the Historic Hatteras Tour, a specially mapped out tour of some of the historic sites from Oregon Inlet to Hatteras Inlet. The second part of the book, the Hatteras Guide, gives you the inside scoop on the attractions, activities, shops, restaurants and places to stay on the island. Whether you're planning a visit or are already here and looking for something to do, you'll find what you need in this guide. It won't take much to get the salt in your blood, in other words, to fall in love with Hatteras Island.

It would be impossible to visit Hatteras Island and not feel the pull of the past. The island's history is palpable and immediately visible in such structures as the Cape Hatteras Lighthouse, the Chicamacomico Life-Saving Station, the skeleton of an old bridge that leads to nowhere, and historical markers by the roadside. But there's much more to the history of the island than you see at first glance. Look a little closer: family cemeteries tucked into crevices all over the island, wooden boats forgotten in creeks and harbors, old homes fixed up or falling down, the old-timers' unusual and charming brogue and the hard-to-pronounce Native-American names for the island locations. Here are clues that there is more than meets the modern eye on Hatteras Island.

Hatteras's history is somewhat overshadowed by the island's new role as a vacation hotspot. Times are changing, and the island will never be the same. But all is not lost. Those who seek out the past and are willing to delve a little deeper into it are rewarded with rich stories and fascinating tales.

Before you go on the tour, take a few minutes to read the history of the island in the Overview and History chapter. Of course we couldn't possibly fit all of the island's history and lore in that short introduction, but it gives you an idea of the chronology of the island's history. The Historic Hatteras Tour route

Photo Courtesy: National Park Service

Fishermen after a haul in Hatteras harbor.

takes you along the entire 50 miles of the island, starting at Oregon Inlet and ending at Hatteras Inlet. If you drive the tour all at once, visiting the sites in chronological order from north to south, expect it to take a good half day, because you'll want to stop along the way to visit the historic sites, scenic overlooks and shops and eat a seafood lunch. You can also do the tour in smaller portions, according to the amount of time you have to spend. Pick an area and explore the historic sites within. We've made the tour easy: The sites on the tour are numbered and mapped to correspond with those on the color maps in the front of this guide.

While you're on the tour, try for a little while to forget the modern world. Try to imagine this island before it was "discovered" by vacationers and recreational fishermen. Stretch your imagination to the time when the oceanfront was barren for the entire 50 miles, save a fishing shack or two. Try to fathom the time when the Cape Hatteras Lighthouse was the only light seen on the entire island. Wrap your mind around the isolation of this island, separated from the rest of the world by miles of open water. Imagine driving in sandy ruts on the beach instead of the secure pavement of NC 12. The photographs in this guide will help you get an image of the way the island was.

But don't get completely lost in the past. Ask questions if you have them.

Notice the care with which old buildings and landmarks have been preserved. Visit the businesses and talk to the people. Explore the present as well as the past.

Keep in mind that a few of the sites on the tour are private residences or on private land. Please, respect people's privacy. We sincerely request that you restrict your tour activities to pausing in front of the building, reading its history and moving on without entering the building or bothering its residents, unless it is a public business or attraction.

We couldn't possibly fit all of the history of Hatteras Island in this small book — and we haven't tried to. Much of the material for the historic tour sites came from Hatteras Islanders who have spent a lifetime, or a significant portion of one, on the island. They shared their memories about the places you will see along the way. Other information came from the countless books that have been written about Hatteras Island. Local bookstores and gift shops and the Hatteras Village Library can steer you to books of local interest. Another way to learn more about the history of the island is to take the Hatteras Bus Tour with local resident Danny Couch (see our Recreation chapter). Couch is a sincere history fanatic and his tours will teach you much about the island.

Have fun, and thanks for answering the call of this island and getting to know it better.

Hatteras Island Then

Captain Pat Etheridge

Photo Courtesy: National Park Service

Hatteras Island's place names provide links to its history. Hatteras, Kinnakeet, Chicamacomico, Avon, Trent, Buxton, Frisco - a lyrical blend of Native American and English words scattered about the island. The most unusual names stem from the Croatan "Indians," members of the Algonquin tribe and full-time residents of the island long before Europeans ever saw this slender strip of sand. "Hatteras" is an English rendition of a Native American word that meant "there is less vegetation;" "Kinnakeet" meant "that which is mixed;" and "Chicamacomico" meant "place of sinking down sand." The other names stem from English settlers who made their way to the island in the 1700s, forming a short-lived melting pot of cultures similar to other colonial areas on the East Coast.

The Croatans were the only Native Americans to live year round on a barrier island. Other tribes lived on the mainland and only visited the barrier islands to hunt and fish, but the Croatans, supported by the bounty of the sea and sound and the protection of wooded areas, found safe haven on Hatteras Island. The Algonquins are believed to have been on the Outer Banks since around 500 A.D.

Native American artifacts are commonly found on Hatteras Island today, especially in Buxton and Frisco. Archaeologists have pinpointed the location of an enormous shell midden (shell repository and trash heap) at Kings Point (now Brigand's Bay) in Frisco, proof that the native population was large and that they had a healthy diet of oysters and clams. Archaeologists now believe that the natives occupied a huge area starting at about the beginning of the Buxton line and ending south of present-day Frisco. Much of this area was part of Buxton Woods. The land under the Cape Hatteras School in Buxton is regarded as sacred by Native Americans.

Other than archaeological remnants, it is only through the eyes of European explorers that we know much about the Native Americans who inhabited the Outer Banks. In 1524 Florentine explorer Giovanni Da Verrazzano, sailing for France, anchored offshore somewhere between Cape Lookout and Cape Hatteras and had a friendly encounter with the native Bankers. All reports of the Native Americans on the island were that they were friendly to European explorers.

The Spanish explored much of this coast before the English, and their maps referred to Cape Hatteras as Cape St. John. English explorers mapped and charted the islands later, and a 1585 English map refers to the island as Croatan Island. John White's map of 1585 first names the cape as "Hattorask."

John White and 116 colonists landed on "Hattorask" on June 22, 1587, and they encountered the friendly natives prior to moving on to Roanoke Island, where they set up a colony. When John White came back to his Roanoke Island colony in 1590 after three years of being away in England, the 116 colonists were gone, the only connection to their whereabouts were the letters "CRO" and "CROATAN" carved into a tree. White assumed this meant the missing colonists had gone to Hatteras to live with the Croatan tribe, but he was never able to go there to find out for himself. We may never know what happened to the "Lost Colonists," but there are some who believe that they did indeed go to Hatteras Island to seek help from the kind natives. Legends of blue-eyed, light-skinned Indians living on the island suggest a mingling of Native American and European genes. And in the 1990s, an archaeologist found a 16th-century English signet ring during a dig in Buxton.

European settlers began making their way to Hatteras Island in the 1700s. These were primarily people of English descent moving to the island from colonies on the Virginia and North Carolina mainland. It appears that Kinnakeet, now Avon, was the first area to be colonized. The first land grant on the island was at Kinnakeet in 1711.

In the colonial period the island was part of Hyde County and was collectively called the Hatteras Sand Banks. The banks were divided into three sections: Cape Hatteras Banks (from old Hatteras Inlet on what is now Ocracoke Island to the cape); Kinnakeet Banks (from the cape to Chicamacomico Banks); and Chicamacomico Banks (through Chickinacommock, or New Inlet, on Pea Island). At this time the banks were heavily forested with live oak and Atlantic white cedar, locally called juniper.

The early settlers only sparsely populated the island. They lived a subsistence lifestyle, gardening, fishing, hunting and raising livestock to provide food for the table. Windmills used for grinding corn bought on the mainland were spotted at Kinnakeet as early as 1723. The islanders also probably did a lot of beach combing. The major shipping routes between Europe, the Caribbean and the New World ran right past Hatteras Island on the Gulf Stream and Labrador Current. Cargo lost overboard or ships wrecked on the island's dangerous shoals would wash up as bounty for the Bankers.

The 1700s were hard on the Croatan Indians, by then called the Hatteras Indians by the new settlers. The Hatteras Indians were attacked by warring tribes, the Corees and the Machapunga, in 1714,

and in addition they had no defenses against the Europeans' diseases of smallpox and tuberculosis. The native Outer Bankers were reduced to poverty and sickness, and by 1788, the natives had all but disappeared.

By the end of the Revolutionary War, which did not bring much action to Hatteras, settlement was growing on the island, but still the population was sparse. More people were moving over from the mainland, and some new residents were shipwreck victims

Photo Courtesy: National Park Service

Buxton boy on cow patrol.

who decided to stay on the island. Longtime island names like Austin, Oden, Gray, Etheridge, Willis, O'Neal and Scarborough all reportedly owe their Hatteras heritage to shipwrecks.

The residents lived on the soundside of the island, in small villages oriented toward the mainland and away from the harshness of the ocean, surrounded by healthy stands of trees that protected them from the elements. The Bankers were farmers, mariners and livestockmen. They fished for their own sustenance, but commercial fishing wasn't a viable trade at the time. They also cut trees and exported them for use in building houses and ships.

Unfortunately, the combination of logging and allowing livestock to run freely all over the island destroyed much of the island's natural vegetation, leaving great bare spots of sand. The sand blew freely in the constant winds and, at Kinnakeet, began to form great migrating sand dunes that could be quite destructive to property and any remaining plants.

In the late 1700s shipwrecks were common off the North Carolina coast, particularly at Diamond Shoals off Cape Hatteras. Two strong ocean currents, the cold Labrador Current and the warm Gulf Stream, collide near Cape Hatteras, and sail-power vessels had to draw close to the Outer Banks to hitch a ride on either of these currents. This should not have been a problem except that the winds and storms so common to the Outer Banks often drove the ships ashore or landed them on shoals. Plus Hatteras Island was so flat with no visible land-marks that ships often didn't realize where they were until they were running aground on its shoals.

So many shipwrecks occurred off the Outer Banks that salvaging the beach for loot was a viable occupation. Eventually, to keep order among salvagers, wreck districts were established to keep track of the numbers of wrecks, and vendue masters were hired to handle the sale of salvageable goods.

In 1773 a teenager named Alexander Hamilton was a passenger on a ship that nearly sank off Cape Hatteras, and he experienced first hand the danger of the cape's dreaded Diamond Shoals. Seven-teen years later, when Hamilton was the second-ranking member of George Washington's cabinet, he still heard terrifying tales of shipwrecks at Cape Hatteras. In 1789 Hamilton, who is reputedly the one who coined the moniker "Graveyard of the Atlantic," urged Congress to investigate the possibility of establishing a lighthouse on the Hatteras Sand Banks. The lighthouse wasn't authorized until 1794, and it wasn't constructed until 1802. Mariners were not impressed with the lighthouse, which they said was not sufficiently bright or reliable.

In 1812 shipwreck victim Sarah Kollock Harris found herself on Kinnakeet Banks in contact with the native residents. Harris, the wife of a North Carolina judge, had this to say about the Hatteras islanders: "The wretches on this island are a disgrace to humanity. I could not have believed that so much depravity was in human beings. Exulting in the calamity which has thrown us among them, though pretending to sympathize in our distress, they would steal the wet clothes which we took from our backs and hung out to dry, and everything belonging to us which they could lay their hands on." Let's hope she just ran into a few bad seeds.

In an 1846 hurricane, a new inlet opened on Hatteras Island, which caused Hatteras Island to separate from Ocracoke Island. Another inlet was also formed to the north — Oregon Inlet, which separated Pea Island from Bodie Island.

Hatteras Inlet brought prosperity to Hatteras Village and doom to Portsmouth and Ocracoke. The new inlet was deep and navigable, and the steady stream of maritime traffic that had always used tricky and unreliable Ocracoke Inlet began to use Hatteras Inlet instead. This brought new work for the people in Hatteras Village as pilots, mariners and boat builders. Island residents also found work in exporting lumber. They cut trees to build boats and houses and to sell. Before the Civil War, live oak was in demand for building Yankee Clippers.

Carolina. In 1861, Confederate troops quickly erected two forts to protect Hatteras Inlet, the only North Carolina passage that could admit large, ocean-going vessels. Forts Hatteras and Clark,

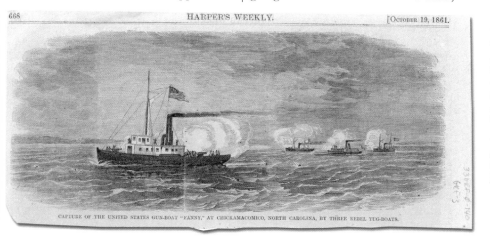

668   HARPER'S WEEKLY.   [October 19, 1861.

CAPTURE OF THE UNITED STATES GUN-BOAT "FANNY," AT CHICKAMACOMICO, NORTH CAROLINA, BY THREE REBEL TUG-BOATS.

The 1850 census provides a clue as to how many people were living on the Hatteras Sand Banks: Buxton - Cape Hatteras: 661 people, 84 of them slaves; Kinnakeet: 318 people; Chicamacomico: 206 people. This meant almost half the population lived around Buxton, west of the cape. There were two new lighthouses on the Outer Banks, a replacement for the old one at Cape Hatteras and a new one south of Oregon Inlet. At this time, present-day Rodanthe and Waves were known as Chicamacomico, Salvo was Clarks, north of Avon were Little Kinnakeet and Scarborotown, Avon was Big Kinnakeet, Buxton was The Cape, Frisco was Trent and Hatteras was Hatteras.

Hatteras Island played a large role in the early Civil War. Both the North and the South recognized that whoever controlled Hatteras Inlet would control the sounds, rivers and seaports of North

on the eastern bank of the inlet, were completed in July of 1861. Only a month later, Federal forces under General Benjamin Butler appeared and bombarded the forts. In only one day of fighting, the Federal forces had control of both.

The Union forces pillaged the island, taking livestock, produce and whatever they could from the islanders to stock the forts. Many islanders fled to the mainland, but others stayed behind. To keep the Federals off their backs, really just for ease of living rather than support of any cause, 111 islanders claimed loyalty to the Union. Because of their loyalty to Union, North Carolina cut off all supplies and trade between Hatteras Island. But the islanders' weren't starving. Many of them found jobs working for the Union soldiers.

The visiting soldiers marveled at the native Outer Bankers. "The islanders mingle little with the outside world. Apparently indifferent to this outside sphere, they constitute a world within themselves," wrote one. Another wrote: "Most of them were born here, never saw any other locality and all are happy. There are women here who have never wore shoes. The people seldom see money, indeed they have no use for it."

After the Civil War, Hatteras Village, because of its deep inlet, grew to be the second leading port in North Carolina, next to Wilmington. The inlet served the inland communities of New Bern, Washington, Edenton, Elizabeth City and Plymouth. It was a prosperous time that sparked the building of many of the historic homes in Hatteras Village. Residents of the other villages sailed to Hatteras Village for their supplies. In 1870, Dare County was formed and included Hatteras Island, which had previously been a part of Hyde County.

Despite the lighthouses to help keep ships on course, wrecks were still happening in alarming numbers off the Outer Banks. In 1874, the first seven Life-saving Stations were built along the N.C. coast, including one at Chicamacomico and one at Little Kinnakeet. That same year, a U.S. Weather Station was also established at the Cape Hatteras Lighthouse. Later, new Life-saving Stations were establsihed at Oregon Inlet, Pea Island, New Inlet, Gull Shoal, Big Kinnakeet, Cape Hatteras, Creed's Hill and Durants (Hatteras Village). The Life-saving Stations, in addition to lighthouses, weather stations and post offices, provided jobs with steady pay, and the islanders scrambled to get them. The Life-saving Stations got the island's first telephones in 1885.

Commercial fishing was also becom-ing a profitable occupation as the locals began to figure out ways to export their catches off-island. People realized that fishing could be a source of income, not just a means of getting food on the table. Islanders fished for finfish, oysters, clams, scallops, turtles, seaweed, whales and porpoises. Porpoise fishing was quite lucrative for a number of years, and there was a porpoise factory in Hatteras Village from 1885 to 1891.

The locals also worked as market hunters, selling ducks and turtles on the market to New York City. When wealthy sportsmen discovered Hatteras Island's incredible hunting potential (a good day's kill was 40 to 50 ducks and geese), they built hunt clubs along the banks. One of the largest was the Gooseville Hunt Club on 1,500 acres near Hatteras Village, but there were others scattered around the island. The locals worked as caretakers at the clubs and took the people hunting for birds and sometimes wild boar. They carved decoys out of old Life-saving Station telephone poles and driftwood and made sink boxes, skiffs and push poles. The Migratory Bird Act of 1917 changed all that, however, outlawing market hunting and placing restrictions on the number of birds shot in one day.

Schools built in the villages helped increase literacy along the banks. Each village had its own schoolhouse attended by children of all ages. Schools, churches and the occasional general store were the centers of island social life. All of the island's small schools consolidated in the 1950s in Buxton.

Cars came to the island around 1915, the same year the Life-saving Service became the Coast Guard. A doctor came to the island in 1923 to work at the Navy

Men taking a break at the CCC camp in Buxton in 1938.

Photo Courtesy: National Park Service

radio station and give medical assistance by radio to men at sea. This one doctor, Dr. Folb, also served the people in all six villages and the eight Coast Guard stations. The main cases he dealt with were tuberculosis, typhoid fever, typhus fever and diphtheria. Throughout the history of the island, there are legendary tales of several midwives who assisted in the births of all the local babies.

A native Hatteras Islander, Con Farrow, remembered the 1920s on the island in a 1976 interview. He said the islanders had no radio, no TV and little communication with outside world but they were happy. They lived in tune with the natural world: "You could listen to the ocean's roar and tell pretty well what direction the wind would be the next day." Everyone had a garden, hogs and knew how to fish. Animals roamed freely. Access to food, building materials and clothing was difficult. Medical care was nonexistent and education was hard. The islanders were self-sufficient. They all went to church and depended on each other's support. There were no taverns and no need for police. No one had

electricity. Hatteras Village got electricity in the mid-1930s, but the rest of island had to wait until the early 1950s.

The Great Depression was a very grim time on Hatteras Island. Livestock was dwindling, hunting laws were strict besides there being a shortage of waterfowl, shipwrecks were rare, boat building was nonexistent and maritime traffic was slow because of better ports at Wilmington and Morehead.

About the same time, a group of people introduced an idea to give new life to the Outer Banks. These people proposed establishing a national park, the first national seashore, on the Outer Banks, including Hatteras Island, to draw tourists to the area. At first everyone supported the idea, especially the poor residents of Hatteras Island.

To protect the area that would be the park, the powers that be brought in Civilian Conservation Corps (CCC) camps to build a protective barrier of dunes along the oceanfront. In 1935, the N.C. General Assembly, in an effort to protect their newly formed dunes, outlawed free-roaming livestock, which was a blow to the residents' way of life and made them suspicious of the new park. In June 1935, 999 acres, including Cape Point and the area around Cape Hatteras Lighthouse, were donated as the nucleus for the national seashore park. In 1937 the park was established and a committee began searching for more land donations. The next year, 1938, Pea Island National Wildlife Refuge was established on the northern end of the island. But all plans for the park were put on hold with the advent of World War II.

In 1942 Germany sent its U-boat submarines to the poorly guarded Eastern Seaboard of the United States. During the first half of 1942, the German subs sank more than five dozen vessels in N.C. waters. Cape Hatteras earned the moniker "Torpedo Junction." Burning ships, gunfire, oil-polluted waters, debris and dead bodies washing up onshore were common sights for the locals.

By the time the war was over, the idea for the national seashore was dead. Oil companies came to Hatteras Island and began buying up rights to drive test wells. The islanders' hopes for the park switched to dreams of becoming rich off the oil prospects. However, the oil companies found nothing and moved on. But a North Carolina Representative reactivated the park project when an anonymous donor gave $618,000 for the cause. The park was finally established in 1953 and dedicated in 1958, preserving more than 60 percent of the island, though many locals felt they were forced to sell their land and not paid nearly enough.

The island's paved highway, N.C. 12, was not completed until 1952. Until then, people drove down the beach or on sand trails on the "inside" of the island. The paved road changed the island, making it easier for its residents to travel between the villages and to the consolidated school in Buxton. It also made it easier for visitors to come in. After a brief ferry ride across Oregon Inlet, Hatteras Island was open to more than the most intrepid visitors for the first time.

When the Herbert C. Bonner Bridge was completed in 1963, Hatteras Island was changed forever. Vacationers have been streaming onto the island ever since. The first large-scale development, Hatteras Colony in Avon, was planned in 1962 by a Northern developer who heard that the bridge was coming and saw an opportunity. He bought 38 oceanfront lots at a price of $150,000. Forty years later, the island is experiencing its biggest real estate boom ever, making millionaires out of investors, most of them not local. Hatteras Island is no longer just a vacation paradise, it's also a real estate investor's dream.

The native islanders have mixed feelings about the easy accessibility of the island. On one hand, their isolation has been invaded. The older the resident, the more harsh the sting of change seems to be. On the other hand, bridges and roads provide opportunities the island has never before known. Young people no longer have to move away to make a living. Jobs are plentiful most of the year. Medical facilities and services are available that weren't dreamed of in years past.

As you tour Hatteras Island try to appreciate all of its past. We'll try to take you there by showing you where to look and providing the old photographs, facts and memories to make it seem real. ℰ

Hatteras Island Driving Tour ❧

1. Oregon Inlet

The expanse of water that separates Hatteras and Bodie islands, Oregon Inlet was formed during a hurricane in 1846. At the time of its formation, the inlet's southern banks were not Hatteras Island but Pea Island. At that time, Pea Island was a small island just north of Hatteras, separated from Hatteras Island by New Inlet. When New Inlet closed, Pea Island became a part of Hatteras Island, but the old name still has stuck.

For nearly seven decades, Oregon Inlet made it impossible to travel to or from Hatteras Island by any other means than boat. The natives traveled to the mainland or Manteo on the mailboat or in their own sailing skiffs. In 1924 Capt. Jack Nelson of Colington opened up access to Hatteras Island by starting a ferry service across Oregon Inlet. He simply towed a small barge behind his fishing boat. Nelson's operation only lasted a couple of months, but soon Capt. Toby Tillett of Wanchese took over and performed the Oregon Inlet ferry service for 25 years. Many longtime visitors still remember the difficult adventure of backing off the ramp of the little ferry into the sand.

In the 1950s, after the Cape Hatteras National Seashore was established, the North

Directions:

The tour begins on the north end of Hatteras Island on the Herbert C. Bonner Bridge over Oregon Inlet. This is at Mile Marker 25 along N.C. Highway 12. Of course you can start at the southern end of the island, at the Graveyard of the Atlantic Museum in Hatteras Village. Just flip to the end of this chapter and remember to reverse all directions.

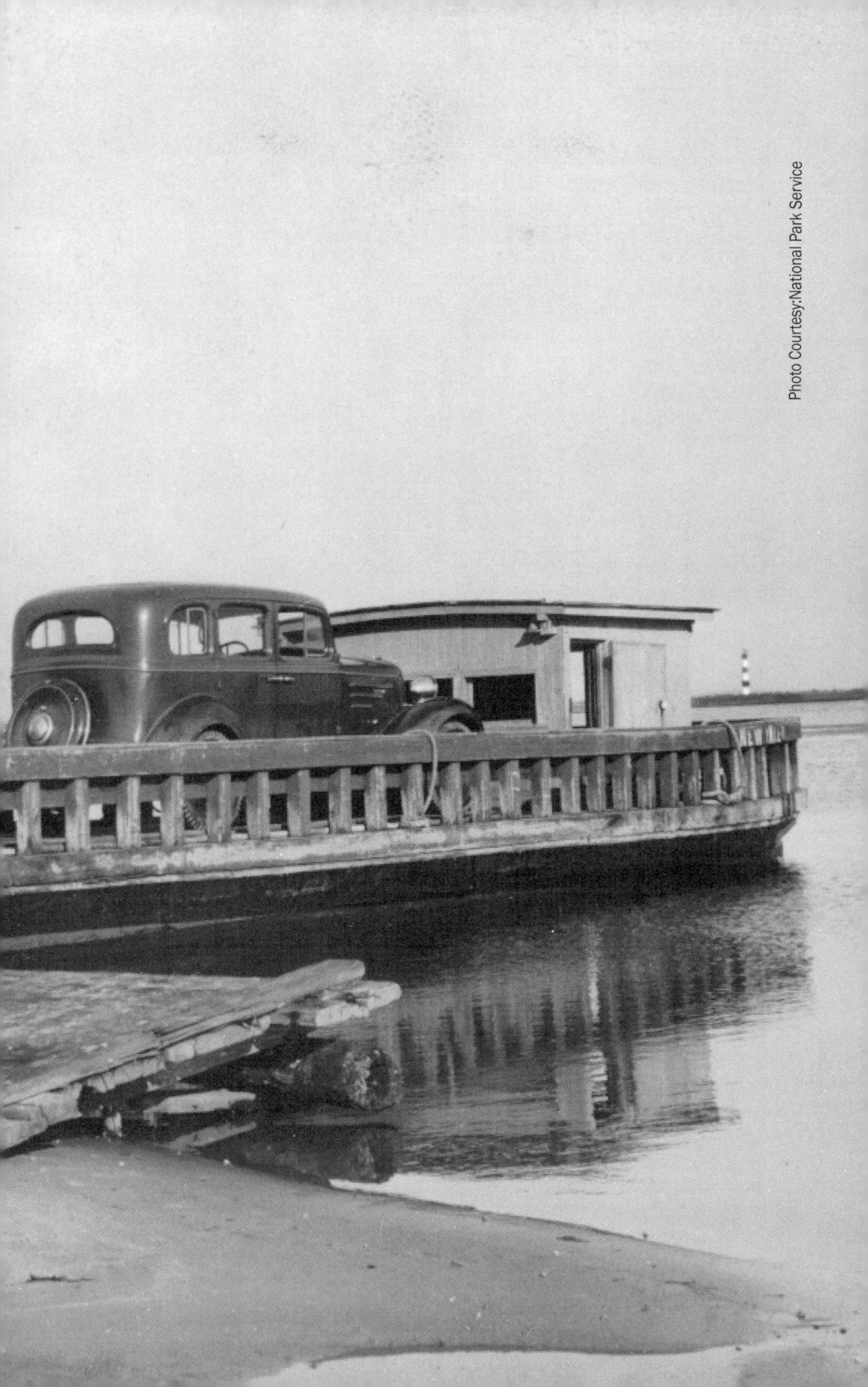

Photo Courtesy:National Park Service

Carolina Highway Department bought out Tillett's ferry service and used old Navy landing craft to shuttle visitors across the island. But visitation was high and even ferries on the half-hour had trouble keeping up with the summer traffic. Soon there was talk of building a bridge across Oregon Inlet so that the visitors could get to Hatteras Island and Cape Hatteras National Seashore. The Herbert C. Bonner Bridge was built in 1963, and a stream of visitors has been flowing across the bridge ever since. The high-rise bridge changed Hatteras Island dramatically, making it a veritable vacation destination.

2. Old Oregon Inlet Coast Guard Station

This elderly building, worn by the ravages of weather and time, was once a proud new Life-Saving Station built to guard the north end of Hatteras Island. This is not the first building to stand here.

In 1896, the Oregon Inlet Station was completely destroyed in a storm. The new station, the one that still stands today, was

Directions:

After crossing the bridge, turn left (east) into the first parking lot. You can park and walk over the dunes for a closer look at the old Coast Guard Station, but you cannot go inside.

The crew of the Oregeon Inlet Station in the life boat around 1945.

completed in 1898. The building came into the hands of the U.S. Coast Guard in 1915, when the Coast Guard took over all the duties of the

Life-Saving Service. The Coast Guard remodeled and modernized the building in 1933-34, and in 1979 the extension was added. Still, the old cisterns used to collect rainwater in the station's early days were left in place. The Coast Guard was still using this building as late as 1988, when it was abandoned because of the threat of being swallowed by the ever-southerly-migrating Oregon Inlet. The rock wall that was built here in the late 1980s has kept it from washing completely away. The new Oregon Inlet Coast Guard Station, on the north side of the inlet behind the Oregon Inlet Fishing Center, was opened in 1992. This old station building is now in the hands of the state, awaiting its future orders.

The Oregon Inlet Station crew with the beach cart, around 1900.

Post Card: Courtesy Outer Banks History Center

3. Former site of the Bodie Island Lighthouse

Somewhere along the southern banks of Oregon Inlet stood the first Bodie Island Lighthouse. Plans for constructing the Bodie Island Lighthouse began as early as 1837, to guide mariners along the stretch of darkness north of Cape Hatteras Lighthouse. A site was selected on Bodie Island, but it wasn't until 1847 that construction was ready to begin. The year before, however, Oregon Inlet opened, separating the selected location from Bodie Island. Despite protests from the lighthouse inspector, the U.S. Lighthouse Board stood by its plan and built the lighthouse in the originally chosen location, even though it meant that the Bodie Island Lighthouse was actually built on Pea Island. The 56.5-foot tower was poorly designed and unstable and soon

Directions:
Go back to N.C. 12 and take a left to head south down Hatteras Island.

after its completion it began to lean toward the sea. In less than 10 years, the Lighthouse Board had to go back to Congress to ask for $25,000 to build another beacon at Bodie Island. The second Bodie Island Lighthouse, also on the south side of the inlet, was completed in 1859. It was 80-feet tall and outfitted with a third-order Fresnel lens.

Two years later, during the Civil War, Confederate troops stacked the new tower with explosives and blew it up, rendering it useless to the Federal forces that were in control of the Outer Banks inlets. By 1871, when the lighthouse was ready to be rebuilt for the third time, the Lighthouse Board decided to locate the Bodie Island Lighthouse north of Oregon Inlet, actually on Bodie Island. Oregon Inlet, which was (and still is) slowly migrating to the south, was within 500 yards of the old site, so the Lighthouse Board wisely moved it to the north side of the inlet, where it still stands and operates today. The former site of the lighthouse is underwater by now, after more than 150 years of the inlet's southerly migration.

4.N.C. Highway 12

Prior to 1952 your trip down Hatteras Island would have been bumpy ride on sand roads, fraught with possibilities of getting stuck. After disembarking from Toby Tillett's ferry across the inlet, you would either have boarded the Midgett family's Manteo-Hatteras Bus - the only public transportation ever on Hatteras Island - or driven your own vehicle down the desert-like stretch before you. You could choose from two main routes. "Riding the wash," driving on the firmest sand of the beach right beside the breaking surf, was the preferable

MANTEO HATTERAS BUS

This areial of Oregon Inlet and north Hatteras Island taken in the 1950s shows the ferry landing, Oregon Inslet Station and the various track roads.

route if the surf wasn't too wild. On the beach you'd encounter nothing but sand and shorebirds and shipwrecks sticking up out of the sand, which you had to be very careful to avoid.

Or you could go on the "inside road," on tire-rut tracks running down the interior of the island. Locals say it was best to always follow the most recently made tracks, no matter where they led. On the inside road you'd pass the island's seven villages. It was a slow trip down the island, especially the 50 miles down to Hatteras Village. The inside road followed about the same line as the Coast Guard's telephone poles.

The Manteo-Hatteras Bus line, which was started in 1938, was a great asset to the people of Hatteras Village, who could then leave the island without traveling by boat or mailboat. The bus line ran regularly for 35 years, until the early 1970s when the paved road and bridge phased

Before the paved road locals said it was best to always follow the most recently made tracks, but people did get stuck.

out the need for the bus. There are many stories of the bus getting stuck in the sand, and even a few about it being almost swept away by the ocean.

The North Carolina Highway Department began paving the "Hatteras Highway" in 1947, starting with a 17.3-mile stretch from Hatteras to Avon, which they finished in 1948. The next stretch - 17.8 miles from Avon to Rodanthe - was completed in 1952. The last 12.4 miles from Oregon Inlet to Rodanthe was finished in the summer of 1952. The paved road brought more and more tourists, and with that, for the first time, the residents of Hatteras Island needed some kind of law enforcement. They had never had the need for a sheriff or policeman before. When island resident Raymond Basnett went to the Dare County Commissioners to ask for an officer, they appointed him deputy sheriff, a position he stayed in for 28 years. In 1961, the island got is first Highway Patrolman.

Directions:

Continue heading south along N.C. 12. As you drive, notice the wall of dunes built up between the ocean and road.

5.Oceanside Dunes

The high row of barrier dunes built up along the Outer Banks oceanfront might seem like a natural part of the Outer Banks environment. From the Currituck Outer Banks through Ocracoke Island, the dunes form a barrier, most of the time preventing the Atlantic Ocean from spilling over onto homes, hotels and roads. But these dunes are not natural elements of the Outer Banks landscape. The dunes are completely artificial, manmade attempts to control Mother Nature.

Prior to these dunes being built, the appearance of the Outer Banks was much different. Old-time Hatteras Sand Bankers say the island

A panorama of Hatteras Island looking north before the dunes were built.

was flat from sound to sea in most areas and that the white beach sand stretched far back into the interior of the island, especially on the north end through Rodanthe and Avon. In most any storm or nor'easter, the ocean water, or "sea tide," washed clear across the island, often into the villages. This saltwater overwash (in addition to free-roaming livestock's eating habits) kept vegetation on the east side of the island to a bare minimum.

In the 1930s, a group of Outer Bankers devised a plan to vitalize the Outer Banks into a thriving tourist attraction. In addition to building a national seashore park, part of the plan was to begin an erosion-control and sand-fixation program to remedy the severe erosion of the Outer Banks beach and ocean side.

In 1936-37 hundreds of the New Deal's Civilian Conservation Corps (CCC) workers came to the Outer Banks to begin construction on more than 100 miles of oceanfront dunes from Corolla to Ocracoke Island. Camps were set up

Photo Courtesy: National Park Service

CCC workers building a dune south of the Cape Hatteras Lighthouse.

Photo Courtesy Outer Banks History Center

A close up of the vegetation fence used to make the dunes.

Directions:

At Mile Marker 31, you'll see large ponds on the western side of the road. Pull into the Pea Island Visitor Center parking lot.

along the Outer Banks to house the workers, including one at Buxton. The CCC workers built the dunes by erecting sand fences and planting small shrubs that trapped blowing sand and began to form small dunes. Once the dunes began forming, the workers planted sea oats and other plants, which have long roots that hold the sand in place. The area from Chicamacomico to Kinnakeet got extra protection with a primary and secondary dune line built side by side. You can still see traces of the secondary berm between Salvo and Avon.

To keep all the new plantings in place, the State of North Carolina outlawed free-ranging livestock so they wouldn't eat up all the plants. The plan worked in preventing ocean overwash: The dunes are still standing seven decades later in all but a few areas; they allowed the re-establishment of local vegetation behind the dune line and allowed N.C. 12 to be built; and they set the stage for ocean-front development along the banks.

But the dunes changed the Outer Banks ecology. Environmentalists say the artificial dunes create an imbalance in the ecosystem, hampering the natural dynamics of a barrier island. The lack of ocean overwash, said to be a necessity in a barrier island ecosystem, is believed to be contributing to the narrowing of the islands by increasing soundside erosion. Thus, the National Park Service no longer rebuilds the dunes when they are wiped out in storms.

6. Pea Island National Wildlife Refuge

In 1937 the Pea Island National Wildlife Refuge was established on a 13-mile-long, 5,384-acre stretch of land on the northern end of Hatteras Island. The area was historically used for waterfowl hunting (the Pea Island Gunning Club was here), life-saving (the Pea Island Life-Saving Station was here as well), farming, commercial fishing and raising livestock. But in 1937 the U.S. Government also saw it as a good place for a wildlife refuge, seeing as its location is right along the Atlantic Flyway migration route. In the early 1950s the refuge staff built 1,000 acres of waterfowl impoundments that support enormous concentrations of ducks, geese and swans every winter. Today the refuge has a bird list that boasts more than 365 species and a wildlife list with 25 species of mammals, 24 species of reptiles and five species of amphibians. There are shorebird nesting areas; wading bird rookeries; nesting, resting and wintering habitat for migratory birds; and habitat for endangered and threatened species like peregrine falcons, loggerhead sea turtles and piping plovers. The name Pea Island is believed to derive from wild peas that grow here, which is another reason it's such hotspot for birds. Since New Inlet closed, Pea Island is not really an island but a part of Hatteras Island.

Directions:

From the Pea Island Visitor Center parking lot, walk across the highway and over the dunes to the beach. At the top of the dunes look out into the ocean to see the remains of the Oriental shipwreck.

7. Oriental Shipwreck

The rusty boiler and smokestack peeking out of the ocean look like evidence of some strange underwater factory, but they're the remnants of the *Oriental*, a ship that wrecked on the bar more than 140 years ago. The *Oriental*, launched on September 18, 1861, was a 218-foot steamer with both sail and motorized power that could carry 100 passengers. At the outbreak of the Civil War, the U.S. Army rented the ship at a price of $1,000 a month; her first military duty was to take the 47th Pennsylvania Regiment from New York to Key West. On its second voyage, the *Oriental* headed from New York to Port Royal, South Carolina, transporting 30,000 letters to Union soldiers and many "Gideonite" missionaries who were going to South Carolina to take care of the newly freed slaves. But along the way, a storm developed and blew the *Oriental* off course, grounding her on the sandbars off Bodie Island on May 16, 1862. Life-saving stations were not established at this time, so the *Oriental* had no one to look to for help. A passenger reportedly rowed a canoe all the way to Fort Hatteras at Hatteras Inlet (at least 40 miles) in the storm to seek assistance in the shipwreck. The Union soldiers at Fort Hatteras came to the aid of the *Oriental* and all of the passengers and crew survived, but the ship was lost. The steamer George Peabody came to take all of the survivors back to New York.

8. Pea Island Life-Saving Station

Directions:
Around Mile Marker 32.5, about five and half miles south of Oregon Inlet, is where the original Pea Island Life-Saving Station stood.

The Pea Island Life-Saving Station was one of 11 stations built along the Outer Banks when the Life-Saving Service went through a second wave of expansion in 1878. The station was authorized on June 18, 1878. It was situated closer to the Pamlico Sound than to the ocean.

In 1879 a British ship, the *M&E Henderson*, wrecked near the Pea Island Station. While four of the crewmen on the *Henderson* drowned, the survivors made their way to the station where they found all of the life-saving crewmen asleep. Thus, the entire crew was fired. The Life-Saving Service then made a move it had never made before: The all-white crew was replaced by an all-black crew, and the USLSS's first black keeper,

Photo Courtesy: Outer Banks History Center

Some of the Pea Island crew with their life boat in the 1940s.

Richard Etheridge, began work on January 24, 1880. The Pea Island Station gained notoriety as the only all African-American Life-Saving Station then Coast Guard Station in the United States. Until then, blacks had served in the Life-Saving Service along with whites, on what were commonly called "checkerboard" stations. But because of racial prejudices, mixed stations were difficult for the African-American crewmen; they were always serving in the lowest jobs.

In May 1880, a month after the crew had gone home for the off-season, the Pea Island station was destroyed by a suspected arson fire. The entire station was destroyed except for the stable, so when the crew came back in the fall, they had to sleep in the stable while the station was rebuilt. No one was ever charged for starting the fire.

The Pea Island crew is most well-known for its rescue of the E. S. Newman in 1896, when Richard Etheridge was still keeper. The ship wrecked on an extremely stormy October night, and the rescue seemed impossible. Ordinary men would have given up. The ocean was too rough to use the life boats or typical rescue equipment, but the crewmen of the Pea Island Station risked their lives to swim out to the ship, tethered by a rope to the shore, and rescue its passengers, one by one, until everyone was saved. The crewmen of the Pea Island Station were not recognized for their valor until 100 years later, when the Coast Guard posthumously awarded them the Gold Life-Saving Medal, its highest peacetime honor.

The Coast Guard took over the station in 1916. By 1931, the old station had been abandoned and new quarters were provided on a site two miles south of the original. The station was decommissioned in 1949 and for a while was used as headquarters for the Pea Island Refuge. In the 1960s, the main 1931 station, lookout tower and cistern were purchased and moved to Salvo to be used as a vacation home. You can see them on the sound in Salvo, the home of Hatteras Watersports.

9. New Inlet Bridge

You could call this the "Bridge to Nowhere." These old wooden bridges once spanned New Inlet and were the only way to get down Hatteras Island. The land on which you now stand is a weak spot in the barrier island, a historical site for a sound-to-sea breach known as an inlet. The name "New Inlet" first appeared on maps in 1738. The namesake is obvious: When the inlet opened it became the "new" inlet and the name stuck. New Inlet was passable, but vessels were reportedly lost on New Inlet's shoals in 1789 and 1836. The inlet got much

Directions:
Near Mile Marker 34 you'll see a small parking lot and boat ramp on the sound side. Pull into the lot or slow down (if you don't have a line of in-a-hurry-drivers behind you) to see the remnants of an old bridge.

The New Inlet Bridge was only used for a few years.

Photo Courtesy: National Park Service

weaker and shallower in 1846 when mighty Oregon Inlet opened nine miles to the north. By 1922, it was closed for good, and Hatteras Island gained about nine miles in length.

In 1933, a hurricane reopened the inlet, forming two separate channels through the island. Hatteras Islanders, who'd gotten used to traveling the new length of Hatteras Island to the Oregon Inlet ferry, were trapped - they could no longer drive any farther north than New Inlet. Narrow, wooden bridges were built across New Inlet, allowing vehicle traffic across the water. You can still see the skeletons of the two distinct sections. Soon after the bridges were built, though, the inlet closed up again and the bridges were no longer needed. Will a bridge be needed here again someday? Possibly, for historical inlet sites have a tendency to reopen. At least six different inlets have been open at one time or another between the location of the Bodie Island Lighthouse and Rodanthe. All it

The New Inlet Station and crew before 1916.

takes is one big hurricane.

A Life-Saving Station was built a half-mile south of New Inlet in 1892. It was moved several times due to ocean overwash and the formation of sloughs in this low area. The beach eroded so much here that the station was eventually stranded on a low, marshy island surrounded by deep channels, which made patrols impossible. The station was finally decommissioned in 1916.

10. Rodanthe/Chicamacomico

Today's Rodanthe is yesterday's Chicamacomico, an Algonquin word supposedly meaning "sinking down sand." Though the Native Americans named the area, the English settlers continued to use the word "Chicamacomico" (and dozens of derivations: Chickony-Commock, Chichinnacomoc, Chick, etc.) to describe the northernmost end of Hatteras Island - the Chicamacomico Banks. The area was populated by English settlers in the mid to late 1700s. By the late 1800s there were distinct settlements on the Chicamacomico Banks. Present-day Rodanthe and Waves were lumped together into one settlement called Chicamacomico. In 1874, when a U.S. Life-Saving Station was established in the northern-most settlement, it was named Chicamacomico, but a post office established here the same year was named Rodanthe. Presumably Chicamacomico was too hard to pronounce or spell for the postal service, but no one seems to remember where the name Rodanthe came from. From then on, the village of Chicamacomico was separated into two sections: North Rodanthe and South Rodanthe. The "North" was dropped when South Rodanthe's name was changed to Waves.

Rodanthe was hit hard in the hurricane of 1899, one of the worst in the history of the Outer Banks. After the storm, several of the Rodanthe residents relocated to Roanoke Island, some of them floating their homes across the sound with them. There are homes in downtown Manteo today that once stood on Chicamacomico Banks.

Rodanthe is on a portion of Outer Banks that sticks the farthest out into the sea; it is the easternmost point of North Carolina. Until the middle of the 17th century there was a prominent cape here, called Cape

Directions:
At Mile Marker 39 is the village of Rodanthe.

Featured Restaurant:
• Leonardo's Pizza ..... page 143

Featured Shopping:
• Hatteras Island Watersports .... page 111
• Hotline Thrift Shop .. page 116
• Island Gift Shop ...... page 117
• The Fishin' Hole .... page 119

Featured Accommodations:
• Midgett Realty .... inside front cover
• Sun Realty .... page 172
• Surf or Sound Realty Ltd. .... page 172A

This cottage located on Uppowoc Street in Manteo was relocated from Chicamocomico after the storm of 1899.

Photo Courtesy: Michael McOwen

Kenrick. The cape eroded away, but remnants of it are just off shore and known as Wimble Shoals. Before the oceanside dunes were built in the late 1930s, Chicamacomico Banks was as flat as a pancake with little vegetation. The beach sand spilled over the entire east side of the island, and the islanders lived as far to the soundside of the island as they could. Because the island is so narrow here, this wasn't very far. The residents of Chicamacomico Banks were plagued with constant flooding.

Directions:

About a half-mile into the village, turn right onto Myrna Peters Road.

11. Rodanthe Community Center

The Rodanthe Community Center, on the corner of N.C. 12 and Myrna Peters Road, was formerly the town's schoolhouse. The schoolhouse has been remodeled to become the Community Center. The children of Rodanthe, Waves and Salvo attended Rodanthe's schoolhouse until all of the island's small schools were consolidated at Buxton in the late 1950s. Salvo native Edward Hooper remembers riding a bus up the road to the Rodanthe School in the 1930s.

A crowd celebrating Old Christmans in Rodanthe.

Photo Courtesy: Outer Banks History Center

He says the schoolhouse had three rooms and outdoor toilets that were freezing in the wintertime.

Rodanthe's Community Center has traditionally served an especially interesting purpose as the location of the village's Old Christmas Celebration, an event that has been observed in Rodanthe for well over 100 years. Old Christmas is celebrated on January 5. About 10 days after the typical American Christmas, the people of Rodanthe traditionally gathered for another celebration that included a gathering with people all of the community plus people from Waves and Salvo, an oyster shoot, a parade, dancing, a feast and, in later years, a settling of grudges. In the old days, the people would dress up in disguise and go from house to house. Another Old Christmas tradition was the appearance of Old Buck, two men in costume impersonating a bull. There's a legend about how the Old Buck appearance started. Supposedly, during a storm, a black and white bull washed ashore as the only survivor of a shipwreck off Rodanthe. The bull became a beloved animal in the village and sired many calves. Each year on January 5 he was led through the village, allowing children ride on his back. But one day "Old Buck," as he was known, wandered off to Frisco and was killed. The villagers created a replica of the beloved bull with a steer's head, a wooden frame and a blanket to cover the two men who walked under the wooden frame. Old Buck has made an appearance on January 5 ever since. The festivities still go on today, though not in the grand character they once did.

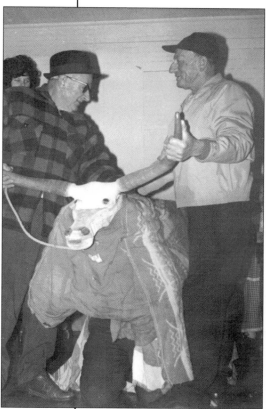

Photo Courtesy: Outer Banks History Center

The replica of "Old Buck" still makes an appearance on January 5th.

Directions:
Drive down to the end of the Myrna Peters Road to the water.

12. Rodanthe Harbor/W.P.A. Camp

The Coast Guard had Rodanthe's tiny harbor constructed in 1936-37, just down the road from their Chicamacomico Station. The Coast Guard also had a channel dredged that led from Rodanthe harbor to the deeper parts of the sound. Until the channel and harbor were built, getting to Rodanthe by boat was difficult because of shallow water, and people just anchored their boats as close as they could get to shore and waded in. The channel and harbor made it easier to get supplies to the Coast Guard Station as well as to the temporary Works Progress Administration (W.P.A.) camp that was located near here during the Depression.

Photo Courtesy: National Park Service

The WPA operation in Rodanthe was based on barges. The camp could be relocated to remain close to where the dune building was being undertaken.

The W.P.A. boys' main job was to hand out food and supplies that the government sent to the people of Hatteras on a regular basis, such as apples, oranges, rice, sugar, raisins and oil. The W.P.A. workers also drained ditches to reduce mosquitoes and cleared and stabilized the sand roads as much as they could. The harbor and channel were an asset to the community members as well. Commercial fishermen still use the harbor today. The little fish-house docks that stand here now are a haven for a colony of very healthy looking cats.

Photo Courtesy: National Park ServiceImage

13. Live Oak Camp / Chicamacomico Races

In this general soundside area in 1861 began a famous Civil War blunder known as the "Chicamacomico Races."

Federal forces from Fort Hatteras at Hatteras Inlet walked to this area of Chicamacomico at the command of Union Colonel Rush Hawkins and set up Live Oak Camp, in an attempt to thwart a supposed attack by the Confederates, who had been forced off Hatteras Island and were now based on Roanoke Island. Two days behind the men, the Union sent a supply ship, Fanny, to Live Oak Camp with supplies and drinking water. Confederate leader Colonel A. E. Wright heard about the Union ship in the area and became convinced that the Union was planning an attack on his troops on Roanoke Island. He sent out his defensive ships, known as the Mosquito Fleet, and succeeded in taking the Union's Fanny, securing about $150,000 worth of gear and all of Live Oak Camp's drinking water.

Levene Midgett at the scales and Charlie Midget, both of Rodanthe, weighing blue fish at the Rodanthe boat house following an early morning seine net haul in Pamlico Sound.

It was the first capture of a Union warship by Confederate arms in the Civil War.

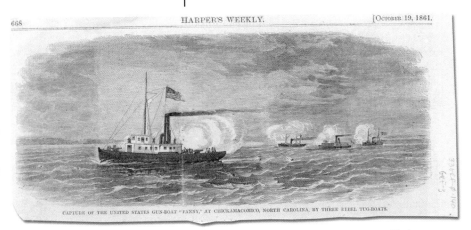

668   HARPER'S WEEKLY.   [OCTOBER 19, 1861.

CAPTURE OF THE UNITED STATES GUN-BOAT "FANNY," AT CHICKAMACOMICO, NORTH CAROLINA, BY THREE REBEL TUG-BOATS.

The prisoners from the Fanny told the Confederate leader about the troops stationed at Chicamacomico, and the Confederate colonel began to plan an attack. Thus began a series of mishaps and bumbling strategies that led both the Union and Confederates up and down Hatteras Island on two blistering hot October days. The Confederate plan was this: Land a Georgia regiment to the north of the federal camp and a North Carolina regiment to the south, close in and secure the enemy, then march south to destroy the Cape Hatteras Lighthouse and march farther down to Hatteras Inlet to take back forts Hatteras and Clark. Things didn't exactly work out that way.

When the Georgia regiment landed to the north of the Live Oak Camp, their boats got stuck in shallow water and they had to walk several hundred yards to land - within full view of the Union camp. The Union commander could also see the North Carolina regiment coming in from the south. But instead of retaliating on these easy targets, the Union commander decided to retreat, leading his men down the island back toward Fort Hatteras. The Georgia troops from the north were close on the heels of the Union, but they gave the Union a lot of headway when they stopped to raid Live Oak Camp. The Confederates chased the Union soldiers, who had no drinking water at all, 25 miles down the island. Meanwhile, the North Carolina regiment that was supposed to surprise the Union soldiers from the south never found a spot to land, though both the Union and Georgian Confederates were fully expecting them to. The chase continued until darkness fell. The Union soldiers made it all the way to the Cape Hatteras Light-house, where they found drinking water and stopped for the night. The Georgians camped nine miles north.

In the morning, the Confederates continued their chase. When they got to the lighthouse and saw the Union camp but no backup from their North Carolina comrades, they turned around, hastily retreating back up the banks to Chicamacomico. The Union soldiers then began to pursue the Confederates back up the island! The Confederates were fired upon by a Federal ship, but no one was hurt. In the end, the Confederates got to their boats anchored at Chicamacomico well ahead of the Union and made a safe getaway back to Roanoke Island. The Federals made it back to Chicamacomico but soon went back to Fort Hatteras. The Chicamacomico Races - after a 60-mile trek up and down the Hatteras Sand Banks - ended up with both sides exactly where they started.

The newspaper captioned this illustration as follows:
The lighthouse at Cape Hatteras round which the 20th Indiana regiment bivouacked after their march of 25 miles from Chicamocomico, on the night of Friday, October 4, 1861.

Image Courtesy: National Park ServiceImage

Directions:

Turn around in the harbor parking lot and head back down the road to N.C. 12. Go across the street to the Chicamacomico Life-Saving Station. If the station is open, we recommend taking a tour.

14.Chicamacomico Life-Saving Station

The Chicamacomico Station was the first life-saving station on the Outer Banks and, miraculously, it is the most intact station left on the Outer Banks. The original 1874 station is the small, ornate building closest to the ocean. Its style is a combination of Carpenter Gothic and the Stick Style. Notice the intricate wooden ornamentation - this was typical of the Carpenter Gothic style and was crafted with the era's new steam-powered saws. Each of the stations built in this style was similar in overall size and appearance, but each had its own unique detailing. The station was originally built three-quarters-mile north of here; it was moved in 1903.

A new Chicamacomico Station was built in 1911 because the original station was too small to house the crew plus

the modern boats and life-saving equipment. The new station, the biggest of the buildings on the compound today, was about a quarter-mile south of the old station, so they moved the old station down the beach beside the new station to serve as the boat house. Due to the threat of erosion, the boat house was moved again in 1959. There are several small outbuildings on the complex. Immediately north of the main station is the 1911 cookhouse. Next to it are two wooden cisterns and a brick cistern that collected rain water. The building west of the

main station is the paint-storage building, while
the next three buildings near N.C. 12 were used
for storage, a stable and a garage. The station was
decommissioned in 1954. The Chicamacomico
Historical Association acquired the property in
the 1970s and worked hard to restore it, preserve
its important history and open it as a museum. It
is on the National Register of Historic Places.

Image Courtesy: Outer Banks History Center

The Chicamacomico Station was most well-
known for its rescue of the British tanker Mirlo
on August 16, 1918, during World War I. German
submarines lurking off the coast of Cape
Hatteras in an attempt to disrupt U.S. shipping
torpedoed the Mirlo, causing it to split in two and
spill burning oil into the Atlantic. Some of the
Mirlo crew made it into lifeboats, while others
were clinging to a capsized lifeboat inside a ring
of oil burning on the water. The Chicamacomico
crew tried several times to launch their motorized
surfboat into the pounding surf and finally
succeeded on the fourth try. The life-savers spent

The crew of the Mirlo *after their rescue on the steamship* Legenia *bound for Norfolk.*

Photo Courtesy: National Park Service

six hours rescuing the Mirlo crew, including the men inside the ring of fire. Ten of the Mirlo's crew died, but 42 were rescued. The British government awarded the Chicamacomico station a gold life-saving medal, and 12 years later the crew received the Grand Cross of the American Cross of Honor.

The crew of the Chicamocomico Station and others at the presentation of American Crosses of Honor in Manteo, July 23, 1930. L to R: Leroy Midgett, Prochorus O'Neal, Zion Midgett, 3 unknown, John Allen Midgett, Aurthur V. Midgett and Clarence E. Midgett

Directions:
Keep heading south down N.C. 12.

15. Waves

You'll hardly notice when you've left Rodanthe and entered the village of Waves. There are no signs delineating the tiny village's boundaries. One of three villages on the Chicamacomico Banks and formerly known as simply "South Rodanthe," Waves got its name in 1939 when the village got its post office. The postal service was notorious for changing names of locations, and it is supposed that Waves got its name from the obvious ocean reference. Other historic names for this village have included South Chicamacomico and Southern Woods.

Directions:
The next site is at Mile Marker 41.

Featured Shopping:

Featured Restaurant:

16. Hatteras Island Surf Shop

This was not the island's first surf shop, but it is a longtime landmark of Outer Banks surfing and one of the pioneers on the Hatteras Island surfing scene. The earliest surfers on Hatteras Island found boards in 1962 and had the island's breaks entirely to themselves. Buxton resident John Conner joined them in 1964. Conner remembers surfing in a sweatshirt and long pants when the water got cold, because they had no wetsuits then. By the mid-1960s, surfers from Virginia Beach had discovered Hatteras Island. Conner opened the island's first surf shop in a mobile home in 1968. In 1969, *Surfer* magazine did a feature on the waves of the Outer Banks, and that was the beginning of it all (the beginning of the end, said local surfers who were used to having the place to themselves). Hatteras Island Surf Shop opened in 1971. The Eastern Surfing Association began holding its annual championships at the Lighthouse in 1972, further exposing the area to surfers from along the East Coast.

Photo Courtesy: Michael Halminski

The Hatteras Island Surf Shop in the 1970s.

17. Salvo

Originally known as Clarks or Clarksville, this village's name was changed to Salvo when the post office was opened here in 1901. There's a legend as to how the name Salvo came about. It's said that a Union ship proceeding north from Fort Hatteras sailed by this village during the Civil War and that the commander of the ship inquired about its name. He was informed that the village had no name on the Union charts. The commander reportedly told the assistant to "give it a salvo (a firing of the cannon) anyway," and the name Salvo was marked onto the Union charts. The name was apparently perpetuated on other maps as well so that when the postal service was looking for a name other than South Rodanthe it chose Salvo. Gull Shoal Life-Saving Station was located in Salvo from 1878 to 1940 and was known for many heroic rescues, especially when Rasmus Midget single-handedly rescued 10 people from the sinking Priscilla in 1899.

Featured Recreation:
• Hatteras Island
Surf & Sail .... page 111

FeaturedAccommodations:
• Camp Hatteras .... page 167
• Outer Beaches Realty
.... inside back cover

Directions:

This one is a little hard to find. It's around Mile Marker 43, about a quarter-mile past the Salvo Market. Look for a little white building with red and blue trim on the west side of N.C. 12.

18. Salvo Post Office

People always make the joke that the Salvo Post Office is the size of a postage stamp. The building is, after all, only 8 feet by 13 feet, reportedly making it the country's smallest post office when it was in operation. The Salvo Post Office was originally built in 1901 up the road where the Salvo Market and gas station is now located. When it was first in operation, mail still came to the island by boat. The mailboat couldn't come all the way to shore because the sound is so shallow close to shore, so the postmaster had to go down to the sound and row, walk or take a horse out to the mailboat to pick up the mail. Later, the mail came by truck across Oregon Inlet.

The Salvo Post Office had only four postmasters in its 91-year history: Mr.

Post Card: Courtesy Outer Banks Historyu Center

The Salvo Post Office.

Kenneth Pugh, Mrs. Marcie Douglas, Mrs. Melvina Whidbee and Mr. Edward Hooper, who still lives on the island today. The tiny Salvo Post Office was so small it was simply towed on a trailer to each postmaster's home. Mr. Hooper took over as postmaster in September of 1979 and moved the building to his yard, where it still stands today. In 1992, the post office was burned by an arsonist and the residents of Salvo rallied to save it. "The men of the village came together and took it apart piece by piece," said Hooper. "Eighty-nine percent of the old floor is from the original building, and most of the framing from the old building is in this one." The people built it back to look exactly like the original. But when the post office was rebuilt, the postal service refused to reopen it because it lacked modern amenities like a bathroom, air-conditioning and a wheelchair accessible ramp. Postmaster Hooper was relocated to the Rodanthe Post Office, where he worked for two more years before retiring. The Salvo Post Office is on the National Register of Historic Places. You cannot go inside the building, but Mr. Hooper doesn't mind if you stop in front of the post office to have a look.

19. Little Kinnakeet Life-Saving Station

The Little Kinnakeet station was one of the original U.S. Life-Saving Service stations built on the Outer Banks in 1874. The smaller building at the back of this site is the original station. Made of pine, the board-and-batten structure was painted a bright vermillion when it first opened. It is like the Chicamacomico station in size and style, a blend of Carpenter Gothic and Stick Style, but it has its own unique ornamentation and detailing. When it was built, the station was much closer to the beach and north of this location.

A chimney was added to the little station in 1884, and a new roof and pantry were added in 1885, the same year the station got a telephone. The separate cookhouse and dining area were added on site in 1892. In 1894, the station and cookhouse were moved away from the ocean, toward the sound, and a little farther south. This was useful, however, because contrary to popular belief, much of the life-saving crews' work was on the soundside, assisting ships, mailboats and local residents who ran into trouble on the sound. They also assisted in fire fighting and other village emergencies. Some of the families of the crewmen built up a very small homesteading village near the Little Kinnakeet Station.

Directions:
Continue driving south along N.C. 12. At Mile Marker 52, about 9 miles south of Salvo, seemingly in the middle of nowhere, you will see a sand road on the right, or west, side of the highway. Turn right here. You can park near the road, or drive farther in on the road, depending on your vehicle. The sand on this trail is firmly packed in some places but deep and soft in others. If you are in a two-wheel drive car, do not drive in any sand that looks thick and deep. Park on hard-packed sand and walk back to the buildings instead.

The Little Kinnakeet station was condemned in 1899, and plans for a new station began. The new station was built in 1904 on a lot one-quarter mile south of the site the buildings had been moved to 10 years earlier. The old buildings were moved down alongside the new building, a 1904 Quonochontang-type bungalow (the bigger building on the site today). The new station had six rooms, including a crew bedroom, an assembly room, an office, a keeper's room, a large closet, an entire second floor dedicated to storage and a watchman's tower.

Photo Courtesy: National Park Service

Little Kinnakeet   Looking N. E.   5/2/35

The old station became the boathouse, garage and stable. Manson Meekins, whose father was chief officer at Little Kinnakeet, remembers the station's "government horse" as a huge, white beast named Old Crowley. He thinks the horses must have been Clydesdales or a similar breed, they were that big.

The Coast Guard took over the station in 1915 when the Life-Saving Service became the U.S. Coast Guard. It was decommissioned in 1938 and the crew was moved to the Big Kinnakeet Station. In late WWII, it was reactivated as a lifeboat station, but it was decommissioned again in 1954. The National Park Service is restoring the buildings and hopes to reopen them to the public as a museum.

Featured Restaurants:

20. Kinnakeet/Avon

Avon was historically known as Kinnakeet, a name that is still often used to refer to the older part of town. Kinnakeet got its first post office in 1873, but 10 years later the postal service

Directions:
Continue driving south along N.C. 12 to Milepost 54

renamed it Avon. In 1850 there were 318 residents of Kinnakeet, and around the turn of the century there were about 500, all of them living on the west side of the island.

The area of Hatteras Island on which the village sits was known until modern times as Kinnakeet Banks. Two life-saving stations anchored Kinnakeet Banks - Big Kinnakeet Station south of the village (about where Hatteras Realty is now) and Little Kinnakeet Station north of the village. The early Kinnakeeters, in the early 1800s, cut down large quantities of live oak and cedar trees and used them for building boats or exported them for use in building ships elsewhere. They basically stripped the island clean of trees. Kinnakeet was known for building small schooners, and in the years following the Civil War it was known for its locally built oystering fleet.

The entire eastern side of Kinnakeet Banks was a flat desert of white sand, and it's said you could see all the way across the island from the sound. The village, even though it was on the west side of the island, was very vulnerable and exposed to ocean overwash during storms. Manson Meekins, who grew up in Avon in the 1920s and '30s, says the sea tide would wash through the village two or three times a year, wreaking havoc on village homes and salt stunting all the gardens. People's homes were built on pilings or had drain holes cut right into the floor.

21. Old Kinnakeet Area

This is the oldest part of the village, where all the families of Kinnakeet/Avon historically lived. Many of the island's most historic and beautiful homes are located back in this area. Manson Meekins, who was born in Avon in 1916, says the village of Avon had 10 general stores to serve 500 residents in the early 20th century. He also remembers that the village, though small, was

Featured Services:
- East Carolina Bank .... page 86
- Kinnakeet Shores Resort Real Estate Company .... page 84 A
- Ocean Atlantic Rentals .... page 113

Featured Recreation:
- Sailworld .... page 113
- Village Video .... page 107
- Windsurfing Hatteras ...... page 112

Featured Shopping
- Ocean Annie's .... page 120
- Askin's Creek Store .... page 127
- Dockside Hatteras .... page 121
- Homeport Gifts .... page 123
- Island Spice and Wine .... page 122
- Kinakeet Corner .... page 124
- Mad Mad Hatteras .... page 125

Featured Accommodations
- Avon Motel .... page 160
- Avon Cottages .... page 170
- Colony Realty .... page 170
- Hatteras Realty
.... page 171 and back of Avon Map
- Midgette Realty . Inside Back Cover
- Outer Beaches Realty
.... Inside Back Cover
- Sun Realty .... page 172
- Surf or Sound Realty ..... page 172A

Directions:
At the stoplight at Milepost 55.5, turn right (west) onto Harbor Road

divided up into five sections. The South'ard was south of the main village (about where Food Lion is now northward); Pot Head was the southern part of the main village to the post office landing; Dog Ridge was from the post office landing to the present-day harbor; Cat Ridge was north of there and included the fire station; The North'ard (later called Spain) was to the north of Cat Ridge separated by a stretch of marsh. North of The North'ard was Little Kinnakeet Village, a very small enclave of homesteads centered around the Life-Saving Station. The occupants of the sections, says Meekins, were set apart from each other, both geographically and mentally. Meekins, who lived in Dog Ridge, says the kids in Dog Ridge didn't get along with the kids in Cat Ridge. But the residents of all these sections went to school and church together anyhow. Today, the entire village is unified as Avon; no one uses the separate names.

Driving around the old Avon area is a treat. We'll point out a few sites for you, but otherwise

Photo Courtesy: Gloria O'Neal

The old Avon School, currently located behind the fire station.

just drive around and do a little exploring.

As you proceed west on Harbor Road, you'll pass over a barely perceptible hump in the road right before the red fire station. This slight hill is part of a dike that was built around the village of Avon in 1926. The dike formed a low wall that prevented the sea tide from washing into the village. To build the dike, a creek was dug. Both the dike and creek are still there, but they're hidden from plain view by increased vegetation and homes.

If you turn to the right on North End Road you'll head to the former North'ard area. You'll pass the site of the Avon school, which was rebuilt where the campground is now in 1933 after a storm knocked down the old school. You can also see one of the old stores, Mr. Fields Meekins' store, about three-tenths of a mile down the road. It's an old white building with blue trim (there's a speed limit sign in the yard). This road is a dead end, however, so if you go down it you'll have to make a U-turn.

Heading straight back on Harbor Road, you'll see many old island homes. Notice how many of the houses are high on pilings to allow the ocean or sound water to run under them. If you stay on Harbor Drive you'll pass the harbor (see site 22), Kinnakeet Methodist Church (see site 23), the old fire station and more. If you take Williams Drive all the way to the end, look for an old windmill grinding stone leaning against a live oak tree in someone's yard; this is a relic from one of two windmills that stood in Avon until 1915.

22. Avon Harbor

Despite its bedraggled but quaint appearance, Avon Harbor, which includes a small marina, fish houses and docks, is fairly modern. It wasn't dredged and constructed until 1946. Before then, the local residents just anchored their skiffs and boats along the edges of the marsh closest to their homes. But the water is so shallow close to shore that often the boats would have to be anchored a good distance out. Invariably, during storms, the boats would wash to shore or, more disappointingly, away from shore. Mill Landing and Old Creek at the north end of the village allowed deeper water access to the village and a safe haven to anchor in during storms, but it was a long walk for most of the village population.

Directions:

Drive down Harbor Road until it curves around the sound.

Sidenotes ✺

A long time ago, the Hatteras Islanders lived in isolation, in tune with nature and all its elements. The residents of the island developed superstitions and remedies that were passed down through the generations. These superstitions were recorded in several editions of *The Sea Chest*, a publication put out by the Cape Hatteras School students in the 1970s.

Old-time Hatteras Island Superstitions

❦ When the moon is bright it means good hunting.

❦ If you shoot a goose before dawn, you'll kill a lot that day.

❦ Fishermen usually get good catches right before Christmas.

❦ Wind in the east, fish bite the least; wind in the west, fish bite the best.

❦ When you're trout fishing, if you catch croakers first, it's a sign that trout are there.

❦ When there's a milky-looking circle around the moon, it's going to snow or get very cold.

❦ When your feet start getting softer, it's going to get colder.

❦ If you see a dove in the morning, it will rain.

❦ If you kill a spider, it will rain.

❦ When the geese start flying south, winter's coming.

❦ If you have a very hot summer, you'll have a very cold winter.

❦ When wasps are out late in the year, it means it'll be a cold winter.

- If the chinch bugs come out, cold weather is due.

- When you cut your wisdom teeth it means you've lived half your life.

- If you see a rat at dusk, you need to clean your house.

- If your nose itches, somebody is coming to see you.

- If you bite your tongue it's because you've recently told a lie.

- If your left hand palm itches, you will lose money; if the back of your left hand itches you will receive money.

- If you tickle the bottom of a baby's foot he will stutter.

- When a bird flies in the house it is a sign of death.

- If you have a cold, fry onions and vinegar together and put it on your chest.

- For an earache, put a teaspoon of urine in your ear.

- For warts, take a kidney bean, rub it on the wart, go in the back yard and throw the bean over your shoulder.

- If you get a bug in your ear, have someone blow smoke in your ear to get the bug out.

- Pack your feet in onions to draw a fever. The fever will leave the body through the feet.

Sidenotes

Photo Courtesy: National Park Service

A view of Avon Harbor.

Before the harbor, the fish houses and freight houses were out in the sound, built high on pilings in deep water so freight steamers and fishing boats loaded with a day's catch could get to them. The original Avon Fish House, it's said, was built in 1896. Commercial fishermen and market hunters (before the 1930s) could unload their catches at the fish house. A freight boat would come in from some city loaded with flour, animal feed, salt pork and other supplies for the villagers, who would row out in skiffs and bring the freight back in. The freight boat would then pick up a load of fish, ducks or turtles to take back to the city.

Manson Meekins remembers that Clemmie Gray's fish house was the main fish house in the sound when he was a boy in the 1920s. It was offshore in four feet of water across from the current harbor. Meekins remembers his mother sending him out to Clemmie Gray's to pick up dinner. He'd walk to shore, borrow a skiff and shove out to the fish house, where he'd buy "a mess of fish (usually mackerel)" and a 20-pound chunk of ice in a burlap bag. Walking back home, he'd feel the cool ice water melting down his back. Then his mother would fix iced tea and fresh fried fish, a true delicacy.

When the harbor was dug in 1946, larger boats could come in to shore, and the need for fish houses and freight houses on pilings in the sound was gone. When N.C. 12 was paved in the 1950s, the need for freight boats was essentially gone too.

23. St. John United Methodist Church

The United Methodist Church has an interesting history. The congregation had a preacher on the circuit prior to the Civil War but no building. After the war, the congregation made plans to build a church, and an oyster boom in 1879 helped provide the money to do so. The men of the village got boats together and went to mainland lumber mills to collect the materials to build the church. Everyone in the village pitched in to move the lumber from the boats to the site, and the church was built in a few months in 1880. A preacher came on, and they built a parsonage as well. When the congregation decided they needed a bell, they found one on the mainland. A story is told that when the ship that was bringing the bell encountered a nasty storm, the people of the village could hear the bell ringing in the boat as it approached Avon in the rough weather. No one remembers if this is really true or not. Mr. Meekins, who attended this church, says he remembers that the village's free-roaming pigs liked to burrow under the church in the cold months. He remembers hearing the hogs grunting underneath the church floor and millions of fleas in the church yard. The church was badly damaged in a 1960 storm; Mrs. Gloria O'Neal remembers it was a tornado. The church was rebuilt in 1962, and a new bell was added. The original bell can be seen in the front yard by the steps.

Directions:
Stay on Harbor Drive , then turn on McMullen to pass the Methodist Church.

Photo Courtesy: Gloria O'Neal

An old photo of the original United Methodist Church.

Directions:

From Harbor Road, head south down N.C. 12. At Milepost 59, you'll see a soundside recreation area and a sign pointing out "Haulover."

24. The Haulover

Before the dunes were built, this area was low, flat and very narrow. It is also a historic inlet site. The John White maps of 1585 showed an inlet near here, and a 1611 map named the inlet Chacandepeco, a Native American word meaning "shallow waters." By the mid-1600s the inlet was closed, but the island remained extremely narrow at this point. In the 1800s, some enterprising island residents devised a way to allow ships, schooners and boats to be dragged over the island from sound to ocean at this point. Thus, the ships could avoid traveling north to Oregon Inlet or south to Hatteras Inlet to access the ocean, shaving hours off their trips. The system required hauling the ships over land, so first the ship had to be unloaded of its

CONSTRUCTION OF TEMPORARY BRIDGE ACROSS THE
NEW INLET IN EARLY STAGES.

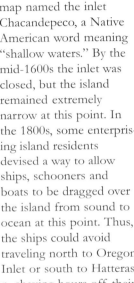

The 1962 inlet at the Haulover.

cargo, which would be transported across the island. Then a team of oxen would pull the ship onto rollers and the ship would be rolled over the land to the ocean. The cargo was reloaded and the ship set out to sea. It's not hard to imagine why people stopped doing this.

The Ash Wednesday storm of 1962 blew out another inlet near here, cutting through N.C. 12 and isolating the southern part of the island. The Highway Department built a bridge across the inlet, but it was only used for about two weeks. Carol Dillon of Buxton says the water through the inlet kept eroding the land from under the north end of the bridge, making it unsafe to cross. So the Highway Department decided to dredge and fill the inlet instead.

NEW INLET WITH CAPE HATTERAS LIGHTHOUSE IN BACKGROUND.

Three views of the inlet formed during the Ash Wednesday Storm in 1962.

In the 1980s, when wind-surfing exploded on the Outer Banks, The Haulover site was a popular spot for the sport. So many Canadians came to windsurf at this spot that the site became known as "Canadian Hole." Many people still call it that.

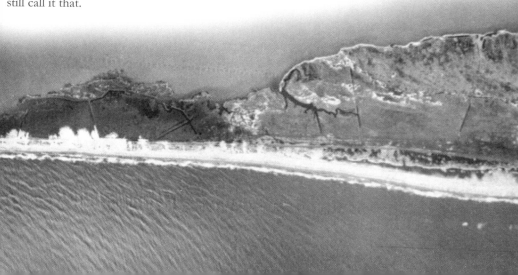

*This rare photo shows the bridge over Buxton Inlet during its brief
existence in 1962 before the inlet was filled.*

Directions:

Two miles south of Haulover is the village of Buxton.

Photo Courtesy: National Park Service

A view of Buxton Village from the lighthouse in 1938.

Featured Restaurants:

Featured Accommodations:

25. Buxton

Immediately west of the coastline's famous Cape Hatteras, the village of Buxton lies on the widest part of Hatteras Island. This section of the island contains something very rare - a densely vegetated maritime forest known as Buxton Woods (formerly known as Cape Hatteras Woods), which stretches through present-day Buxton and Frisco. It is also the highest point on the island. As the highest, widest and most densely vegetated area of Hatteras Island, it is a safe haven that has always been one of the most heavily populated areas.

Native Americans lived year-round through-out this wooded area. It is believed that the Native American colony stretched from the northern end of present-day Buxton all the way through the southern end of present-day Frisco.

The area of present-day Buxton was known to the first English settlers as The Cape. Before the paved highway was built through the island, Buxton's sand roads meandered through the woods under canopies of trees, leading to dwellings, the schoolhouse, general stores and churches. Today, most everything is centered on the main road, but there are still some homes tucked back in the woods. Part of the woods is now the Buxton Woods Coastal Preserve.

A post office was established at the eastern edge of the woods in 1873, and it was named The Cape. The name of the post office was changed to Buxton in 1882. It is said that the name was in honor of a judge, Ralph P. Buxton.

The Cape Hatteras Lighthouse, the Cape Hatteras Life-Saving Station and a U.S. Weather Bureau located out on The Cape historically gave the local residents employment that helped the area thrive. In 1902, inventor Reginald Fessenden transmitted the world's first wireless message from Buxton to Roanoke Island. All of the island's disparate schoolhouses consolidated into one large school in Buxton in the 1950s.

26. Cape Hatteras Lighthouse

Mariners have always feared the passage around Cape Hatteras. Passing by this cape is so dreaded not only because of Diamond Shoals (great sandbars that protrude southeasterly from the cape) but also because the cape marks the convergence of the warm Gulf Stream and the cold Labrador Current into a turbulent collision of water. In the early days of shipping, so many wrecks occurred at Cape Hatteras that the U.S. Government had to do something to protect the shipping industry. The first Cape Hatteras Lighthouse was authorized in 1794, at the urging of Alexander Hamilton, who was then working under President George Washington. The brown sandstone, octagonal lighthouse was not completed until eight years later, in 1802. With the beacon only 90 feet high and not very bright, the lighthouse drew criticism from sea captains. One captain called it "the most important on our coast and without doubt the worst light in the world." After years of complaints, the lighthouse was refitted in 1854 with a new lens and lantern and was elevated to 150 feet. During the Civil War Confederates destroyed the lens and lantern, but the U.S. Government had them restored by 1862.

In 1868 work began on a second Cape Hatteras Lighthouse because it was easier to build a new one than to make necessary repairs to the old one. The new site was 600 feet northeast of the original location. The new lighthouse, 208

Directions:

If you see the old location of the light, take your first left. Then you can go back to the main road and go to the new lighthouse site. Follow the signs leading to the Cape Hatteras Lighthouse.

OLD TOWER, CAPE HATTERAS N.C. OCT. 24 '70
View from the West

A view of the Cape Hatteras Lighthouse, built in 1802 and refitted in 1854.

Photo Courtesy: National Park Service

A view of the Cape Hatteras Lighthouse in 1893 from the beach. It is remarkable how much wider the beach was then.

Notice the large pile of rubble about 600 yards to the south of the lighthouse. Those are the remains of the previous lighthouse that was destroyed when the new one was built.

feet from top to bottom, was lit on December 16, 1870, with the beacon 192 feet above ground. It was, and still is, the tallest masonry lighthouse in America. The old tower was blown up, and nearby residents collected the bricks to use in chimneys and structures around the village. In 1873 the lighthouse was painted with its signature black and white diagonal stripes. Surviving lightning strikes, hurricanes and even an earthquake, the Cape Hatteras Lighthouse continued its duty for another 65 years.

By 1936, ocean waves were lapping at the base of the Cape Hatteras Lighthouse, and though it was still in good condition, it was closed. Carol Dillon, who grew up in Buxton, remembers standing on the base of the lighthouse in the 1930s with the waves crashing around her feet. She also remembers playing in the empty lighthouse with her friends, making as many dashes as they could up and down the 268 stairs. In place of the lighthouse a substitute tower was

C S A CAPE HATTERAS LT STA. N. C. MAY

built on a metal skeleton structure a mile and a half away in Buxton Woods. The light worked, but it was ugly and the residents of Buxton did not like it. The CCC boys, led by W. E. Byrum, made some efforts to build up the dunes and plant trees to prevent the erosion around the old lighthouse.

The erosion control efforts of the CCC worked fairly well, and in January of 1950 the Cape Hatteras Lighthouse was illuminated again. But erosion continued to threaten the lighthouse. Over the years, man's efforts to save the lighthouse from erosion - sand replenishment, sandbags, a groin and rock jetties - could not stop the encroaching sea, but they made for a famous surf break in the 1970s and '80s. After much deliberation on how to save the lighthouse, it was moved 2,900 feet away from its original site in 1999. Its new location is 1,600 feet from the ocean. You can still see the base of the old lighthouse location.

27. Double Keepers' Quarters and Principal Keeper's Quarters

The two well-maintained white buildings on site at the Cape Hatteras Lighthouse served as homes for the light keepers. The buildings were moved to this site when the lighthouse was moved in 1999. The larger of the two, the Double Keepers' Quarters, was built in 1854. It was a duplex, with two exact living spaces on either side, separated by walls for privacy. The principal keeper and his family lived on one side and the assistant keeper and his family lived on the other.

The smaller building, the Principal Keeper's

Photo Courtesy: National Park Service

194. C. S. S. CAPE HATTERAS LT. STA., N. C., MAY 30,1893   DWELLING NO. 2.

The Double Keepers' Quarters in 1893.

Quarters, was built in 1870, at the same time as the new lighthouse. By then, maintenance of the light and the site required three keepers. The principal keeper and his family had this house on their own, while the two assistants and their families shared the big house. The new Keeper's Quarters was built with brick and stone left over from the construction of the lighthouse. Brick walkways surrounded both quarters and were connected by a brick walkway that led to the lighthouse. A white fence separated the two dwellings. Each keeper had a storage shed to store livestock feed and tools. Most keepers had livestock as well as small gardens to supplement their governmental provisions. Each house had a summer kitchen until modern kitchens were installed indoors. Each keeper had an outdoor privy as well as a cool bin for storing perishables. One of the keepers remembered stocking his cool bin full of a very rare treat - bananas - when a freight boat carrying bananas wrecked off the cape in the early 20th century. The keepers' families tell stories of never being lonely or feeling isolated at the Cape Hatteras Lighthouse. There were three families always on site, plus the villagers, Weather Station staff and visitors regularly dropped by to visit.

Photo Courtesy: National Park Service

The CCC cabins located just south of the lighthouse.

28. Former CCC Camp

On your left, in the area that is now wooded, is where Hatteras Island's CCC camp was located in the 1930s. This area was not wooded when the camp was here, says Carol Dillon of Buxton, whose father worked at the camp. Dillon remembers that there were about 12 wooden buildings at the camp - an officers' building, a mess hall, a garage and several barracks for the men. The CCC boys were responsible for building the dunes that line the oceanfront, and they also worked to save the Cape Hatteras Lighthouse from falling into the sea. The W.P.A. crews from Rodanthe and Frisco built a baseball diamond out between the lighthouse and the beach for the CCC boys and

Directions:

Leaving the lighthouse parking lot, turn left onto the curved road to head toward the beach. On the road that takes you out to the beach and Cape Point, you'll pass a few interesting sites along the way.

the Buxton residents to use. Many Buxton old-timers remember playing ball there well after the CCC boys were gone.

29. Graves of British Seamen

On the right side of the road, look for the sign directing you to a very small cemetery. You'll have to park and walk down a short path to the site. These are the graves of two British seamen who washed up on the Cape Hatteras beach after their British merchant ship was bombed by a German U-Boat during World War II. The people of Cape Hatteras gave the two men a proper burial with grave markers and a nice white fence to surround their graves.

During the first six months of World War II, German boats lurking off the North Carolina coast bombed and sank more than five dozen Allied shipping vessels. Some residents of Hatteras Island remember seeing great flames on the sea as oil tankers burned, and they remember having to darken their windows so the lights from their homes wouldn't give the Germans any clue as to where they were. The Cape Hatteras Lighthouse, at that time a substitute skeleton beacon, was darkened as well. Carol Dillon, who was born in Buxton in 1928, said she remembers hearing great explosions in the middle of the day while she was in school and the windows of the school-house shaking like they, too, would explode. She also remembers a time when she and a friend were swimming in the ocean at night and were mistaken for German soldiers coming ashore by the Coast Guard. The Coast Guardsmen warned them never again to come to the beach at night or they might be shot. It was believed that the German soldiers did come to shore at times. There are even tales of the Germans buying supplies like coffee and sugar from fishing boats in the ocean.

30. Cape Point

The paved road ends not quite at Cape Point but close. If you have a four-wheel-drive vehicle you can keep driving on the sand out to the Point, which is a popular surf-fishing spot. The end of the road was the approximate location of the 1882 Cape Hatteras Life-Saving Station, about 1 mile south of the lighthouse. This crew was charged with watching over the most dangerous shoals on the East Coast, Diamond Shoals, and stories about their numerous rescue efforts abound. It was decommissioned in 1941.

Also out here near Cape Point, about one and a half miles south of the lighthouse, was the Hatteras Beacon Light. Built in 1855, it was a small, supplementary beacon to the Cape Hatteras Light-house. Its main purpose was to guide local boats around a turning point on a route from the Atlantic Ocean to the Pamlico Sound through a shortcut from Diamond Shoals. The beacon had a sixth-order Fresnel lens and was only 25 feet tall. The building was a wooden frame box that was painted red with a light on top. A third assistant keeper under the principal keeper at Cape Hatteras Lighthouse manned the station but had to supply his own housing. The beacon was moved three times due to erosion and darkened by the Confederates during the Civil War, but it served mariners until 1906.

Photo Courtesy: National Park Service

The Beacon Light, once located at Cape Point, provided aid to navigation through Diamond Shoals.

Directions:

Go back out to N.C. 12 and turn left, heading south. The next site is around Milepost 61.8 on Light Plant Road across from Conner's Supermarket.

31. The Old Gray House

There are several historic homes in Buxton that were built in the late 1800s and early 1900s. A ride along the main highway and side roads will reveal several that are still standing. The Old Gray House is one such home. We chose this one to show you not only because it has been converted into a retail shop and you can go inside, but also because the current owners – Dewey and Mary Parr – love to tell stories about the history of their home. The Barnette family built this house in the early 1800s, says Mr. Parr, making it one of the oldest homes in Buxton. The exact date is not known because the early nineteenth-century Hyde County property records were destroyed in a fire. The house sat by itself on Dark Ridge Road, without much around it but trees that were so thick you could hardly see the sky. The Gaskins family owned the house next, and then the Gray family bought it. The Grays were Kinnakeeters who, like many other families, left Kinnakeet after a particularly nasty hurricane and flood to seek higher ground in Buxton.

Mr. Parr is the grandson of the Grays. Growing up in Buxton he visited his grandparents' house almost every day, as he passed it on his way to and from the schoolhouse, which was down at the end of the road. (You can see the old school site at the end of Light Plant Road, where the Cape Hatteras Anglers Club is now.) Parr remembers that friends and relatives would gather here often, especially during storms or on winter evenings, to tell stories. "Of course, they were always the same stories," he says. Parr remembers that the community of Buxton was tight-knit. "When I was growing up," he says, "you were everybody's kid. Your feet were welcome under everybody's table."

Stop in the Gray House and Mr. Parr will likely point out the interesting architectural features and historic details of the house.

32. Rocky Rollinson Road

On this road you can get a look at two other historic island homes, which belonged to the Rollinson family. The Rollinson family name dates back to the 1700s on Hatteras Island. The two large white homes with green trim on the left side of the road were built by William "Rocky" Rollinson. The first home was built in 1890. The second of the homes, at 47402, was Rocky Rollinson's own homeplace, built around the same time. Rollinson was a local builder who built homes, boats and public buildings. He constructed the Cape Hatteras Life-Saving Station.

Directions:
Head south again on N.C. 12 and take a right on Rocky Rollinson Road. After you've seen site 32 turn around on Rocky Rollinson Road and head south on N.C. 12.

Directions:
Head south along N.C. 12. Notice the Pilot House Restaurant on your right. This was once Buxton's mail landing and freight boat landing, where everybody in town liked to go. A windmill was also located there.

Joseph Christ Jeanette windmill for grinding corn. It was on the present site of the Pilot House Restaurant

Photo Courtesy: National Park Service

The old Buxton Post Office (above) in an earlier incarnation. In the old days the mail boat would come up the creek near where the Pilot House Restaurant stands today and drop off the mail.

Summer bus trip, 1952.

Directions:

Head down to Frisco, which begins at around Milepost 64.5.

Featured Restaurant

Featured Shopping

Featured Accommodation:

33. Frisco / Trent

Frisco is a small village without a lot of visible historic landmarks, but the history of the area dates back to the Hatteras Native Americans, and some refer to part of this island as Indiantown. At the western edge of the maritime forest, this area is believed to be the border of the Hatteras natives' living area. A great shell midden, or oyster shell and trash repository, was found here at Brigand's Bay (formerly known as King's Point). The midden, which is said to be several football fields long, led some archaeologists to believe that as many as 5,000 natives once lived on the island.

Frisco was called Trent by its first English settlers, and it used to have three large sand hills, called Stowe's Hills, as a landmark. Later, the dominant feature of the landscape was a big hill called Creed's Hill. A Life-Saving Station was established at Creed's Hill in 1879. Longtime residents say they remember the woods in and around Trent being extremely thick and that delicious wild grapes grew on vines in the woods. The post office was established at Trent in 1898, but for some reason the postal service changed the name to Frisco. It is believed that Trent was too close in spelling to the Trenton post office on the mainland. Supposedly the new name was suggested by the town's first postmaster, a man named Wallace who, before becoming shipwrecked on Hatteras Island, spent a lot of time in San Francisco, Calif. In the early 1900s

The original Frisco Post Office.

Photo Courtesy: Outer Banks History Center

there was a yaupon factory in Frisco, with a man by the name of Scarborough using the leaves of the native plant to make tea. Yaupon leaves were first harvested and consumed by the Native Americans. Consumed in large quantities, yaupon tea is a purgative, but in normal amounts it is a caffeinated beverage similar to tea. The early English settlers traditionally drank the tea, but the practice went out of favor as coffee and black tea became more readily available on the island.

Making Yopon Tea:— The sweating Hogshead. Mark or Crane

Photo Courtesy: National Park Service

34. Old Trent Area

A little jaunt down this road will give you a peek into Frisco's past. You'll see several old homes, including a few rundown ones that may not be there much longer. The little orange house immediately on your right was built in 1895 and is an example of a modified Coastal Plains Cottage, a style of architecture you'll see elsewhere on Hatteras Island. When you get to the end of the dirt road, take a right and stop. This east-west road was Trent's main road, one of several that wound through the woods. Notice the big white house on the right, which was built in the early 1900s. Mrs. Mildred Poole, a Trent native in her 90s, says that Trent today is nothing like it was when she was growing up, that all the houses and all the former residents she remembers are gone.

Salina Farrow moved to this area of Frisco in 1935. At that time she remembers that the sand

Directions:

About 3 miles into Frisco, look for a road named Sunset Strip on the west side of the road. Turn onto this road.

Featured Attraction and Recreation:

roads were not named and the people lived very spread out in the woods. Her husband fished and her children went to school in Buxton on the bus. There was one small store, but mostly they went to Hatteras Village for groceries. "There were not many people here because there was nothing to do," she says.

It's best to turn around and drive back down Sunset Strip to N.C. 12, as there's not much to see by heading down the private road except modern homes. The name Sunset Strip didn't come about until the 1960s, it's said, when a group of free-spirited hippies lived back in this area.

Directions:

The next site is at the corner of Sunset Strip and N.C. 12.

35. Frisco Native American Museum

We've directed you here because it is the only place on the island to learn about the history of the Hatteras Native Americans and to see the artifacts collected on the island. But the building that houses the museum has a little history too. According to Grace Peele of Hatteras Village, this building was Ulysses Rollinson's Store, built in the 1950s when the highway was paved through Frisco. The store was actually built using the lumber from an even older store farther up in Frisco village. The store was a popular gathering place, and it later became a shell shop. Now the building is home to the Frisco Native American Museum, a well-loved Hatteras Island museum owned by the community-conscious Joyce and Carl Bornfriend. The

Go inside the unassuming building. You'll find a treasures of Native American artifacts. We promise it will be well worth the visit.

museum houses artifacts from the tribe that lived on Hatteras Island, and the owners are very knowledgeable about Native American history. Interestingly, the Bornfriends found an ancient dugout canoe on their property, and it's on display here. You can also walk on nature trails behind the museum. See the Attractions chapter for more information about the museum, but definitely stop here if it's open when you pass by.

36. Creed's Hill Coast Guard Station

Directions:
Continue driving west on N.C. 12. As you're leaving Frisco look for an interesting gray and white building on the oceanfront at about Milepost 68.5.

The original Creed's Hill Life-Saving Station, built in 1879, is no longer in existence. It was built near Creed's Hill in Trent, about four miles south of the Cape Hatteras Lighthouse, or about three miles north of the site you're now on. In 1912 it was discovered that the Creed's Hill Station had been operating on a site for which the U.S. government had no title or lease. A new site, this one on the ocean across from Sandy Bay, was selected in 1917, when the station had been transferred to the hands of the Coast Guard. This second Chatham-type station was built in 1918. Grace Peele of Hatteras remembers walking from Hatteras Village to the Creed's Hill station to see her father, who worked here. She remembers the great big water tanks, or cisterns, that were at the station and getting a cool drink of water from the tanks by filling a conch shell and taking sips from the shell. The Coast Guard station was abandoned in 1947 and is now in private hands.

Photo Courtesy: Outer Banks History Center

Creeds Hill Coast Guard Station.

Directions:
About a half-mile west of the former Creeds Hill station, about Milepost 69, is the former site of Isabel Inlet.

Photo Courtesy: NOAA

An aerial view of the inlet opened by Hurricane Isabel.

37. Isabel Inlet Site

(Also see the sidebar on page 167)

When Hurricane Isabel roared through the Outer Banks on September 18, 2003, a 1,700-foot-wide inlet opened between Frisco and Hatteras Village and cut off Hatteras Village from the rest of the island. The island on the far side of the inlet became known as "Little Hatteras." Ocean water flowed right through the roadbed to the sound, and the villagers had to boat on and off the island. The schoolchildren were ferried to school on a headboat. There was a little debate about whether to build a bridge or fill the inlet, but filling the inlet won out. The highway was reopened on November 18, 2003, exactly two months after the inlet was created. The U.S. Army Corps of Engineers filled the inlet with 555,000 cubic yards of material dredged from the Hatteras Inlet ferry channel at a cost of $7.5 million. The North Carolina Department of Transportation repaired the 2,400-foot section of road in six days at a cost of $650,000. The road officially opened to the public on November 22, once again allowing access to Hatteras Village and Ocracoke via the Hatteras Inlet Ferry.

An inlet also opened at this exact spot during a hurricane in 1933. The islanders built a bridge to span the inlet, but by the time they were finished with the bridge the inlet had filled back in. Wooden pilings from the old bridge were exposed during Isabel.

38. Durant Point – Porpoise Processing Factory

Durant Point was once the home of a porpoise factory, starting in 1885. The islanders' harvested "porpoise" and processed them to produce oil that they could sell on the market. Photos from the days of porpoise fishing reveal that the islanders were actually harvesting bottle-nosed dolphin.

Porpoise fishing was done out on the beach, where the fishermen would establish rudimentary base camps. They used nets to corral the giant mammals, that traveled in a "wafe" or a school, and dragged them to the beach. One old piece of literature reported: "Catching the fish was easy. Getting them to the market was when the work began." Because the early porpoise fishermen did not have motorized vehicles, they had a lot of work to do to get the porpoise from the beach camps to the soundside factory by horse and cart. The outer skin was used for machinery belts, while the oil was separated from the blubber to be used in the manufacturing industry. The best part of the animal was the jawbone oil, which could reportedly garner $1,000 a barrel. The carcass was used as fertilizer. Porpoise fishing ended on the Outer Banks in the 1920s.

Directions:
Just west of the Isabel Inlet site, look to your right across the bay toward the marshy point of land that juts out into Pamlico Sound.

Directions:
Look to your left as you enter Hatteras Village, to the area where a few hotels and the white sand of the beach greet you.

Photo Courtesy: Outer Banks History Center

Durants Station in 1917

Featured Restaurants

Featured Shopping

Featured Recreation:

39. Former Site of Durants Station and Billy Mitchell Events

Here, on the oceanfront, the Hatteras Life-Saving Station was built in 1878. Its name was later changed to Durants. The original station was decommissioned in 1939 and sold to a private owner. It was converted into a hotel in 1952 and stood on this site until 2003, when Hurricane Isabel washed the 126-year-old building away.

In August 1923, a world-renowned Navy airman named Billy Mitchell established a camp and an airfield near Durants Station. He hired many of the local residents to help him construct the airfield on the sand near the beach and then flew in a crew of Navy pilots to set up a camp out there. The crewmen at Durants Station got a kick out of the outsider men fighting off mosquitoes and trying to set up tents in the Outer Banks wind, but they eventually let them in their station to share their quarters. Mitchell had made good friends in Hatteras Village in previous years during hunting and fishing trips to the area.

Mitchell selected Hatteras Village as a good location to test his theories about naval air power. He was planning to use Navy airplanes to bomb two decommissioned Navy battleships. The activity seems commonplace today, but in Mitchell's time, many people believed that an airplane couldn't possibly sink a battleship. The common belief in that day was that battleships were indestructible. Mitchell had already proven his point once off the coast of Virginia, but he wanted to do it again at Hatteras to prove to naysayers that the U.S. Navy could set up all manner of little airstrips and crude bases along the East Coast and destroy threatening subs and battleship with airplanes and bombs. While Mitchell's men prepared for the mission, their bombs were delivered by ship and sat in crates out on the beach for all the locals to see. On September 5, 1923, Mitchell and his men conducted the tests. A few Hatteras Villagers fled town, thinking the bombs would drop too soon and harm the village. The planes loaded with bombs took off from the handmade sand airstrip and headed to ships that were anchored off Cape Hatteras at Diamond Shoals. It took several attempts but the planes succeeded in sinking the decommissioned *Virginia* and *New Jersey*. That afternoon, the Hatteras Village residents feted Mitchell and the crewmen with a barbecue and feast by the sea.

40. Hatteras Village

Hatteras Village was settled but didn't really begin to grow and prosper until the opening of Hatteras Inlet in 1846. The new, deep inlet lured maritime traffic away from Ocracoke Inlet, and the village naturally grew to accommodate the ships that were passing through Hatteras Inlet from ocean to sound or vice versa. Hatteras Village's post office was established in 1858. Early in the Civil War, the Union got control of two Confederate forts near the inlet, and the village was pretty much taken over by Federal soldiers for the duration of the war. After the war, maritime traffic picked back up through the inlet, and Hatteras Village prospered. Residents of Trent and Kinnakeet moved to Hatteras to work. For a while it was one of the largest ports in the state, the main point of entry for cargo ships headed to mainland communities like Elizabeth City or New Bern. A Life-Saving Station was established here in 1878 and was originally called the Hatteras Station; its name was later switched to Durants because of confusion with the Cape Hatteras Station. Hatteras Village suffered a bit

Photo Courtesy: National Park Service

An old postcard from the Atlantic View Motel.

Hatteras, N.C.   Feb. 21, 1949

You'll cross over this bridge on your way to the next site. Look around and see how things have changed since 1949.

of a decline as the state built major ports at Wilmington and Morehead City, but the residents got by on government jobs, commercial fishing and duck hunting. The town's first hotel, the Atlantic View Hotel, was built in 1928 just east of the village. The 15-room hotel catered to hunters, who had been coming to Hatteras since the late 1800s, and fishermen, who began coming to Hatteras more regularly when sport fishing took off here beginning in the late 1930s. The center of Hatteras Village has always been where it is now, at the crossroads just past Slash Creek Bridge. This area was called "Up the Road" while the area farther down near the harbor was called "Down the Road."

41. A.S. Austin's Store

Andrew Shanklin Austin purchased an acre of land in the heart of Hatteras Village in 1916, and for the next two years he worked on constructing this building. Austin ran a general store down-stairs, selling everything from molasses to baseball bats to meats to kerosene. He also owned part of the shipping company that brought the supplies to the village via a freight boat from Elizabeth City. In the upstairs portion of the building Austin had boarding rooms that he rented out to the village teachers since the Hatteras Village School was directly across the street. It's said that children on the school's ball field were always trying to knock out the store's lights with a long-shot baseball. Storms in the 1930s and '40s caused

Directions:

Continue driving into the village. After you cross the little bridge over The Slash, look for a crossroads and a large white building with a big front porch on your right side.

The AS Austin Store.

flooding in the store, so Austin raised the building 18 inches off the ground in the mid-1940s. Austin's brother "Shank" ran the local movie theater on the lot directly next door (on the east side) from the 1940s through 1960s, and people from all over the island would come here to see the movies. What you see today is still the original building, ship's timbers in the foundation and all, except for the front porches that were added on later. This is the oldest original building still being used in a commercial capacity in the village, says its owner Eddie Skakel, grandson of A. S. Austin.

42. Burrus Red and White

A store has been right on this site in Hatteras Village for almost 140 years. The Stowe family opened Hatteras Store and Co. here in 1866. The Burrus family later married into the Stowe family and brought that name to the business as well. The original ledgers from the early days of business are still around, showing what people bought back then, things like tobacco by the pound, salt pork, calf-skin boots, shot, cloth and pigs. Most of the trading was done by the barter system in those days. It's said that the original wooden store building washed around a little bit in the storms of 1899 and 1933, but it has always been on this site in the heart of Hatteras Village. There have been dozens of stores in Hatteras Village, selling "everything from hair pins to horse collars" says Dale Burrus, who runs Burrus Red and White with his brother Allen today. The current brick store was built in 1946 behind the original store, which was then moved elsewhere in the village to be used as a home. That old building has since been torn down. Burrus Red and White, the only grocery store in town, is still at the center of the village, with people always running in and out or stopping to talk on the porch.

A photo of the Hatteras Store in 1866. Notice the pigs in front of the store

Photo Courtesy: The Burrus Family

Image Courtesy: The Burrus Family

A bill of lading from 1876 showing goods purchased by Mr. Stowe for the Hatteras Store.

43. Cape Hatteras Weather Station

Directions:
The next location is next door to the Burrus Red and White.

Built in 1901, the Cape Hatteras Station was the first official building constructed for the U.S. Weather Bureau. The Weather Station had previously been located at the Cape Hatteras Lighthouse, where it was established in 1874. It then was moved to Durants Life-Saving Station in 1880. In 1883 it was moved to a private residence in Hatteras Village until this building was constructed. This Craftsman-style building is a good example of the early 20th-century style of public buildings and it is the only remaining building from the original Weather-Bureau design.

Photo Courtesy: Outer Banks History Center

The Cape Hatteras Weather Station was the first official building constructed for the U.S. Weather Bureau.

Because of the island's volatile weather patterns, the Hatteras Weather Station developed into an important place for interpreting and forecasting the weather. Staffing the weather station usually required two men, an officer and an assistant. Every hour the men would take readings of temperature, humidity, wind velocity, rainfall and barometric pressure and record these readings into a logbook. The readings were also sent to the Weather Bureau's headquarters in Washington. The weathermen set out warning flags and lights for the villagers who might be venturing out on the water that day. Meteorolo-

U.S.
POST OFFICE
HATTERAS - N.C.

Photo Courtesy: National Park Service

This rare photo shows the Weather Station Outhouse, which was destroyed in 1978. As with the main building, it was the first official Outhouse constructed for the U.S. Weather Bureau.

Directions:

Head down Kohler Road.

gist Richard Dailey, who served as Hatteras' weather expert for 35 years, lived for a long time in this location of the Cape Hatteras Weather Station with his wife and children. The Daileys, because they lived at the Station, had electricity from generators long before anyone else on Hatteras Island did. The Weather Station moved back to Buxton in 1946 because the Weather Bureau (now the National Weather Service, part of NOAA) felt it needed a location on higher ground. This building was later used by the U.S. Coast Guard, three North Carolina colleges and as park service housing.

The National Park Service acquired this building in 1958, and it has been on the National Register of Historic Places since 1978. The Park Service has been restoring the building since 2001 and will open it to the public this year as a weather museum. Most of the original structure has been salvaged, and during restoration logbooks and artifacts were found behind the walls. The yellow and green paint scheme is the same as the original Victorian colors, learned through extensive historical paint analysis. See our Attractions chapter for more about the new museum.

44. Old Hatteras Village Homes

To get a look at some of Hatteras Village's oldest homes, it's nice to drive down Kohler Road and its side streets, where local residents have lived since the 1800s. Driving through here, look for the older homes with little plaques marking their dates. These homes are part of the Hatteras Village Guided Tour, for which there are brochures at locations around town. Two interesting houses can be found by turning left onto Stowe Landing Road and left again onto MV Australia Way. Down at the end of MV Australia Way on the left is the **Ellsworth and Lovie Ballance House**, which was built in 1915, has been restored and is on the National Register of Historic Places. This house was typical of the type of "I" house — a two story, side-gable dwelling with a central hall — built in eastern North Carolina at the turn of the century. Turn around in the cul-de-sac and just before you turn right again onto Stowe Landing, notice the green home on the left side of the road. This is the **Frank Stowe House**, built

Photo Courtesy: Outer Banks History Center

An early picture of the Frank Stowe house.

before 1888. The house was reportedly moved here with horses and rollers and ropes in 1888. You'll notice that Stowe is a popular name on the homes and streets in this part of town. The Stowe family owned a large chunk of land between the sound and sea including this and the center of the village. They donated the land for the town's church and school, which stood where the community center is now on Highway 12.

45. Hatteras Marlin Club

In the 1930s, the first attempts to catch a blue marlin off Hatteras were made by a few visiting sportsmen from the north, but no one succeeded in catching one until 1939, when Hugo Rutherford caught one on his private boat with local captains Lloyd Styron and Hallis Foster at the helm. The first local man to catch a blue marlin was Ernal Foster, the village's first recreational charter boat captain, in 1951. From then on, marlin fishing became more common in Hatteras Village, with out-of-towners coming in regularly to try to catch one of the giant deep-sea fish.

Directions:

Turn right on Saxon Cut, the road that runs between the Weather Station and the Burrus grocery store. The next site is at the end of the road.

Photo Courtesy: Outer Banks History Center

The Hatteras Marlin Club

According to Lloyd Styron, in a *Sea Chest* interview from the 1970s, one of the visiting marlin fishermen, Mr. Walker Wilkins, helped Hatteras fishing guide Edgar Styron establish docks, two charter boats and a restaurant on this site in 1953 to better accommodate visiting anglers. Later, a group of influential anglers who had formed the private Hatteras Marlin Club bought this property from Styron to use as a place to tie up their private boats. These men predicted early on that Hatteras was going to be a great marlin fishery and in 1959 established the Hatteras Marlin Club International Blue Marlin Tournament, which began drawing anglers from along the East Coast and the islands. The tournaments were very successful. Lloyd Styron, who was the tournament's weighmaster for 12 years, said, "Several times we had so many fish hanging on the rack that we had to lay them on the ground. We were afraid the rack would collapse." The day before the 1962 tournament, the world record blue marlin was caught at Hatteras, and at the 1974 tournament 32 blue marlins were brought to

the docks. Sights like this led to Hatteras becoming known as the "Blue Marlin Capital of the World," a name that sticks today. The Hatteras Marlin Club is still a private fishing club. Its annual Blue Marlin Tournament, in its 45th year in 2004, is still held, though it's now a release tournament.

46. Hatteras Harbor

A developed Hatteras Harbor like you see today really didn't come about until the late 1930s and later. Prior to then there was no shoreline development or enclosed harbor, but rather freight houses and fish houses on pilings in the deeper sound water off shore. Some of the offshore buildings were reached by walkways, others by boats or skiffs. This was because the water close to shore wasn't deep enough to allow boats of much size to come all the way in. In 1936, the first shoreline docks were built by Hatteras Development Company, which established the village's first electricity and ice plant. With this, Hatteras Village got electricity before the rest of the island. Rollinson's Channel, which leads from the village to the sound, was dredged so that boats could easily get to the docks. This was the beginning of Hatteras Harbor.

Directions:

Turn around in front of the Marlin Club and head back to Kohler Road. Turn right on N.C. 12 and drive west until you see Oden's Dock on your right.

Photo Courtesy: National Park Service

By the 1950s the harbor consisted of the Marlin Club docks, Oden's Gas Dock and Fish House, and Foster's Quay (see Site 48). Improvements to the channel and harbor were made in 1956, and the breakwater that protects the harbor was built in 1960-61. Today there are seven marinas in Hatteras Village supporting a charter fleet of as many as 35 boats and numerous private boats.

The Oden family business started out with a small fish house and grew slowly as they added a gas dock, marina slips, a restaurant and more. The fourth generation of Odens is now working in this family business. The Oden family's roots in Hatteras can be traced back to a shipwreck in the early 1830s. It is told that John Oden washed ashore at Hatteras in a rum barrel, the only survivor of a ship he had been sailing around the Cape. Since it was the second time he had wrecked on Hatteras, Oden decided that fate must have wanted him there. He married a local woman and stayed.

Directions:

You'll find Foster's Quay right next to Oden's Dock.

47. Foster's Quay / Albatross Fleet

Foster's Quay is the home of the Albatross Fleet, the first charter boats on the Outer Banks. Capt. Ernal Foster launched the original *Albatross* in 1937 and used it to take the first charter fishing parties to the Gulf Stream. That summer he only booked four trips for $25 each. Foster wasn't the first local man to take a fishing party out from Hatteras, but he was the first local to commit to charter fishing first and commercial fishing second. Often he had to travel 25 miles across the sound to pick up his fishing customers in Engelhard because Hatteras Village was so hard to reach via the island's sand roads. During World War II, the Navy requisitioned the *Albatross* against Foster's will and used it in the service, but Foster got it back before going off to war. When the war was over, Foster came back to Hatteras Village to sport fish. He also had to commercial fish to supplement his income, but he was committed to charter fishing. Foster added two more boats to his charter fleet in 1948 and 1952. All three *Albatross* boats were built in Marshallberg, North Carolina, by Willis and Sons boat builders.

Ernie Foster as a boy.

Several notable events happened on the *Albatross* Fleet. In 1951 Foster was the first local man to catch a blue marlin when his fishing party hooked but didn't want to reel in the big fish. In 1952 a woman on his boat, Mrs. Ross Walker of Richmond, Virginia, became the first woman to catch a blue marlin north of Florida. In 1958, Jack and Ellie Cleveland of Greenwich, Connecticut, were the first to catch and deliberately release a blue marlin onboard the *Albatross II*. In that day, the normal practice was to bring the fish in to the docks, where it would eventually rot. The conservationist Clevelands were ridiculed for releasing their fish at the time, but they were contributors to today's practice of catch-and-release. In 1962, the *Albatross II* brought in the world record blue marlin, an impressive 810-pound fish, whose record has since been broken. This fish is mounted on the outside wall of the Hatteras Village Library in the center of town. Ernal Foster and his *Albatross* Fleet were the pioneers of Hatteras sport fishing. The three boats are still running today, with Foster's son, Ernie, at the helm.

Photos Courtesy: The Foster Family

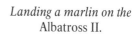

Landing a marlin on the Albatross II.

Directions:
Continue heading west on N.C. 12.
When you get to the stoplight,
head toward the Graveyard of the
Atlantic Museum and park in the
parking lot. Definitely go inside the
Museum.

48.Forts Hatteras and Clark

In 1861, after North Carolina seceded from
the Union, a small fleet of Confederate river
boats was trying to protect all of the inlets on
the North Carolina coast. It soon became clear
to the Confederate leaders that much more was
needed to protect the state's inlets, which were
extremely important to the South's supply routes.
The Confederacy began constructing several
forts along the N.C. inlets, including forts
Hatteras and Clark on the east side of Hatteras

A map from 1861 showing the location of forts Hatteras and Clark on the south end of Hatteras Island.

Inlet in the summer of 1861. At that time
Hatteras was the only inlet on the Outer Banks
deep and wide enough to admit large, ocean-
going vessels, so its forts were extremely
important. Fort Hatteras was the principal fort,
located one-eighth mile from the inlet. Fort
Clark was about three-quarters of a mile east of
Fort Hatteras nearer the ocean. The fort sites
would have been farther west than the museum
parking lot, but they have since washed away.

By the end of the summer the forts were
nearly complete and 580 men were stationed
there, including eight companies of the 17th N.C.
Regiment and the Tenth N.C. artillery. About the
same time a Maine man who had been a ship-

wreck victim at Hatteras and short-time prisoner at one of the forts found his way to the Union commanders and gave them important details of the fortifications at Hatteras. The Union planned an attack. In August 1861 Union soldiers arrived in ships that embarked from Fort Monroe in Virginia. Over the course of two days they succeeded in taking over both forts Clark and Hatteras. It was the Union's first naval victory, and they then had control of all three Outer Banks inlets. The Confederate troops retreated to Roanoke Island. As many as 11,500 Union troops were stationed at the forts by 1862, and their presence was a commanding force in tiny nearby Hatteras Village.

The Union's commanding officer, Colonel Rush Hawkins, cultivated friendly relationships with the people of Hatteras Village. Within 10 days of the takeover, nearly half of the men of the island had pledged their allegiance to the Union. Some say the islanders were neutral but pledged their allegiance to the Union because it was in their favor to do so at the time. In October 1862, 111 citizens of Hatteras Island assembled at a church near the inlet and adopted a "Statement of Grievances and a Declaration of Independence" and loudly proclaimed their loyalty to the United States. They set up a provisional or temporary government with the local preacher Rev. Marble Nash Taylor as governor. The government tried to get a seat in Congress, but they were largely ignored because their jurisdiction was only a one-mile-wide sand island on the N.C. coast. Because of Hattears's loyalty to the Union, the mainland portion of the state cut off all trading with the village. The islanders soon had no flour, salt or other food except for fish and no way to replace them. Word of the pitiable condition of Hatteras's Union sympathizers reached New York, where several philanthropist types, including poet William Cullen Bryant, decided to help them out by sending supplies and food to Hatteras. The people in the North admired the Hatteras

Sidenotes ❧

Right: A model of the Monitor on display at the museum.

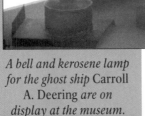

A bell and kerosene lamp for the ghost ship Carroll A. Deering *are on display at the museum.*

The Graveyard of the Atlantic Museum

In the late 1970s and early '80s, when artifacts from the *Monitor* shipwreck were being hauled up from the ocean floor near Cape Hatteras, the people of Hatteras Island were disappointed. The artifacts from the 1862 Union gunboat were carted away from the Outer Banks for restoration and display at the Mariner's Museum in Newport News, Virginia. The shipwreck clearly belonged to the Outer Banks, but there was no place on the islands suitable to house and display them, so it was only right to take them away.

"Wouldn't it be great," people of the Outer Banks thought, "if we had a place of our own to rightfully store and display the artifacts that came from our waters?"

Thus the idea for the Graveyard of the Atlantic Museum was born, and before they knew it, a group of Hatteras Islanders was involved in a major museum project in conjunction with the National Park Service (NPS) and the National Oceanic and Atmospheric Administration (NOAA). The museum's scope grew from one ship's artifacts to 400 years of history and thousands of shipwrecks off the Outer Banks coast.

By the early 1990s, the group had secured a site for the museum from the National Park Service, a prime, seven-acre, oceanfront site next to the ferry docks on Hatteras Island. In 1995 they brought in a paid director and leader, Joseph Schwarzer, to guide the project to fruition.

"When Joe came, all we had was a dream," says Dale Burrus, an original board member of the museum.

Indeed, there was no site plan for the museum and no real vision of how it would raise funds or operate. But during Schwarzer's

General Billy Mitchell on a bombing run off Frisco.

Image Courtesy: Graveyard of the Atlantic Museum

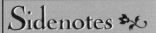

first week of work, the museum got its first grant from NOAA and things were under way. The $7.8 million project made steady progress every year. Already, $5.6 million has been raised for the museum.

The striking, 19,000-square-foot museum building, designed with ship's elements, was completed in 2001 and the interior was finished in 2002. In 2003 the museum opened a portion of its building featuring an exhibit on naval airman Billy Mitchell and a Museum Store.

The entire museum is not open at this time because the organization still needs to raise $2.2 million, but when that goal is met, the museum will be fully operational, housing a collection of artifacts of national and international significance.

"We have a broad range of materials ready to go on display," says Schwarzer. "The frustration is that because of limited funds we

Name plates taken from some of the many ships wrecked on the Outer Banks.

Photo Courtesy: Beth P. Storie

can't get them out there for public view."

It won't be long, we know, before the final dollars are raised and the museum is fully open to the public. At that time, visitors will see artifacts from the *Monitor*, from Blackbeard's ship the *Queen Anne's Revenge*, from the *Carroll A. Deering* "Mystery Ship," from German U-boats and much more. Visitors will learn about the incredible tales of shipwrecks and lifesaving on the Outer Banks.

For now, the museum is open Monday through Friday from 9 a.m. to 5 p.m. (call or stop by to check hours, as they may change in the summer). Visitors can see an exhibit in the lobby and shop in the Meekins Chandlery Museum Store. Sometime this summer the museum will put up an exhibit on the Life-Saving Services and Lighthouses of the Outer Banks. Next year promises an exciting exhibit on the Civil War on Hatteras Island.

Be sure to stop by the museum in Hatteras Village, and, if you can, make a donation. All contributions bring the Graveyard of the Atlantic Museum closer to opening for good. 𝒞

Photo Courtesy: Beth P. Storie

Coins and other artifacts found on Hatteras beaches are on display. Some of the coins found here are more than 2000 years old and originate from places all over the world.

residents for their courage in siding with the Union while residing in a Confederate state. Nearly $8,200 worth of supplies and food were shipped to Hatteras Inlet, but by the time the ship arrived, the locals had found work with the Union soldiers. They sold a great deal of the produce and returned the money to the charitable organization.

49. Hatteras Inlet

For a period of about 82 years, Hatteras Island was joined to Ocracoke Island. Before 1764 the two islands had been separated by Old Hatteras Inlet, which was located midway between Ocracoke Village and the location of the present inlet. When Old Hatteras Inlet closed for good in 1764, Hatteras and Ocracoke were one island and it was possible to travel by land between the settlements on Hatteras Island and Ocracoke Island. That was all changed September 7, 1846, when a storm blew open a deep and wide inlet that became known as Hatteras Inlet. A local man, Redding Quidley, was the first captain to pilot a vessel both on the inbound and outbound routes through the inlet in 1847, and from then on the traffic through the inlet increased. Commercial traffic through the inlet stopped during the Civil War, when the Union had control of the forts along the inlet banks. From the end of the Civil War through 1890, three steamships regularly ran through Hatteras Inlet between mainland North Carolina ports and northern ports like New York City and Baltimore, and commercial traffic through the inlet was brisk. But David Stick's history of the Outer Banks says that the last commercial vessel ran through the inlet in 1895. About that time

Directions:

The tour really ends at the Graveyard of the Atlantic Museum. You can walk or drive around to the ferry docks, if you'd like, to see the inlet, or take the ferry across the inlet over to Ocracoke Island.

Photo Courtesy: Beth P. Storie

The Graveyard of the Atlantic Museum.

there were hopes of making Hatteras into one of the main ports of entry in North Carolina, but the Army Corps of Engineers found too many problems with Hatteras Inlet. Then, when the Intracoastal Waterway was established, Hatteras was bypassed entirely on this important shipping route. The state focused its efforts on the ports at Morehead City and Wilmington. From then on, the inlet was maintained for small boats only.

After World War II, Frazier Peele began operating a ferry across Hatteras Inlet to Ocracoke Island. His ferry could handle four cars, and it's said that he would often shoot ducks and geese from the bow of the en-route

Featured
Ocracoke Accommodation:
Harborside Motel .... page 107

Photo Courtesy: National Park Service

Off to Ocracoke!

ferry. The State of North Carolina bought Peele's ferry in 1957 and has been providing regular trips across the inlet to Ocracoke Island ever since. ?

The Last One Of

Where first-class amenities
environment and the advantages of
all come together in one bea

HATTERAS ISLAND a

AVON PIER

KINNAKEET SHORES OCEAN BEACH CLUB

NC HWY. 12

⬅ MEDICAL CENTER NORTH

HATTERAS REALTY

POST OFFICE

NC HWY. 12

LAKE KINNAKEET

TERN ST.

YUCCA ST.

OCEAN VIEW DRIVE

PAMPAS ST.

ENTRANCE

MYRTLE ST.

SALES & RENT OFFICE

FATHOM LAKE

KEEL LAKE

WWTP MAINTENANCE AREA

NORTHERN BOARDWALK & NATURE TRAIL

LATTITUDE LAKE

FUTURE PLAN

VILLAGE LAKE

PONY PASTURE LAKE (FUTURE PLAN)

PROPOSED ROAD

LAKE MORG

Credits:
Developer: Outer Banks Kinnakeet Inc.
Telephone: 252-995-3511, Fax: 252-995-3512
Email: info@kinnakeetshoresresort.com
Website: Kinnakeetshoresresort.com

Land Planner: Bissell Professional Group, Kitty Hawk, NC
Map Illustrator: Gary Crane, Colington Island, NC

This master plan is a representation only and is subject to change per regulatory approvals.

BIRD & WILDLIFE REFUGE AND FEEDING AREA

BIRD & WILDLIFE REFUGE AND FEEDING AREA

OTTER POINTE

N E S W

PAMLICO SOUND

COMMUNITY

Kinnakeet Shores

Kinnakeet Shores Resort Real Estate Company • Avon, NC • MP 57   (252) 995

One Of Its Kind.

...menities, a pristine natural
...ntages of Hatteras Island ownership
...n one beautiful community.

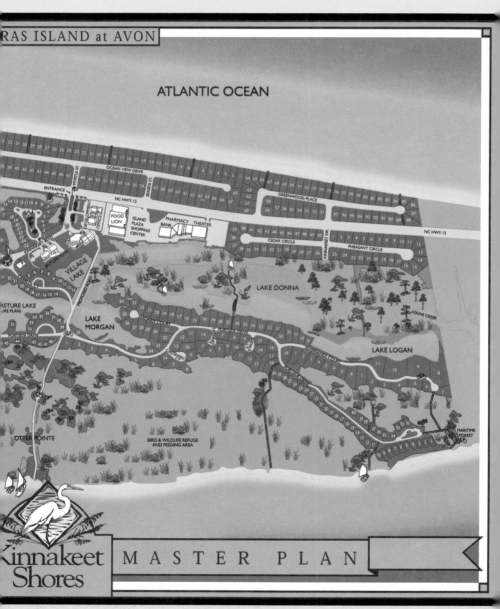

MASTER PLAN

Its Kind.

a pristine natural
Hatteras Island ownership
autiful community.

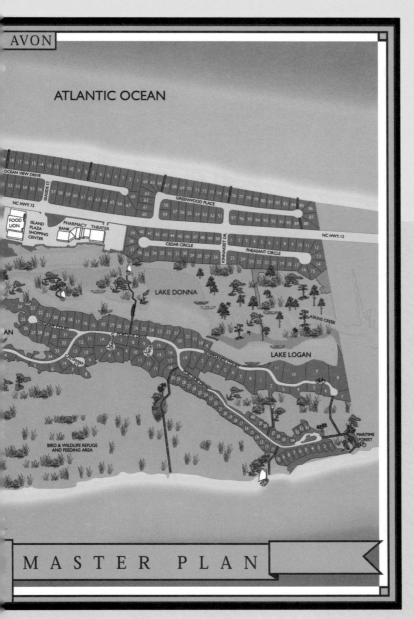

AVON

ATLANTIC OCEAN

MASTER PLAN

The Last

Where first-class a
environment and the adva
all come together i

HATTE

AVON PIER

KINNAKEET SHORES OCEAN BEACH CLUB

NC HWY. 12

⊂⊃ MEDICAL CENTER NORTH

HATTERAS REALTY

POST OFFICE

NC HWY. 12

LAKE KINNAKEET

OCEAN VIEW DRIVE

TERN ST.

YUCCA ST.

PAMPAS ST.

CHANNEL COURT

FATHOM LAKE

KEEL LAKE

WWTP MAINTENANCE AREA

BRIGANTINE

CANNONADE CT.

LATTITUDE LAKE

PONY P (FU

Credits:
Developer: Outer Banks Kinnakeet Inc.
Telephone: 252-995-3511, Fax: 252-995-3512
Email: info@kinnakeetshoresresort.com
Website: Kinnakeetshoresresort.com

Land Planner: Bissell Professional Group, Kitty Hawk, NC
Map Illustrator: Gary Crane, Collington Island, NC

This master plan is a representation only and is subject to change per regulatory approvals.

NORTHERN BOARDWALK & NATURE TRAIL

BIRD & WILDLIFE REFUGE AND FEEDING AREA

BIRD & WILDLIFE REFUGE AND FEEDING AREA

N E S W

PAMLICO SOUND

C O M M U N I T Y

Kinnakeet Shores Resort Real Estate Company • Avon, NC •

Hatteras Island Now ❧

Visiting Hatteras Today

Hatteras Island has changed a lot in the four decades since the Bonner Bridge was built over Oregon Inlet to connect the island with the northern Outer Banks. In that time, visitation has steadily increased so that the island economy is now almost entirely centered on tourism dollars. But the most dramatic changes on Hatteras Island have really occurred in the last five or so years, as developers and stock-market-burnouts-turned-real-estate-investors have scooped up the last remaining island properties and built thousands of new, luxury rental homes, luring more tourists who in turn require more amenities like shopping centers, restaurants and things to do.

Yet the Hatteras villages haven't seen nearly the development of the northern Outer Banks resort towns of Nags Head, Kill Devil Hills, Duck and Corolla. When Hatteras Islanders find themselves complaining about the development on their own island, they often end the conversation by saying "at least we aren't like Nags Head," with a great sigh of relief.

Some of the island natives and longtime residents and visitors are upset about the rapid changes on Hatteras Island, but many locals welcome progress

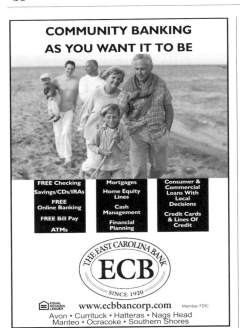
and the increased opportunity it brings. After all, tourism allows many people to live and work in this place that they love. Many of the current Hatteras Island residents vacationed here first then fulfilled a dream to move to the island when work became available. This was easier to do five years ago, however. Since then, real estate prices have skyrocketed.

And the development on Hatteras Island can only go so far. Sixty-three percent of the island is federal park that will never be developed, while another 14 percent belongs to the state and another 11 percent is wetlands. This leaves only 12 percent of the island open to private ownership and development.

The permanent, year-round population of Hatteras Island is around 4,000. The island residents are independent yet tight-knit, eager to help each out in the face of hurricanes and other hardships. There are two schools on the island – Cape Hatteras Elementary and Cape Hatteras Secondary (middle and high school combined). Both schools are in Buxton and draw students from all seven of the island villages.

For outsiders and visitors, Hatteras Island will always be a heavenly retreat far removed from the rest of the world. Visitors welcome the chance to enjoy this long, thin island that offers access to sea and sound, and more than three million of them visit Cape Hatteras National Seashore every year. The seven island villages maintain their quaintness and charm, thanks to Cape Hatteras National Seashore, which contributes greatly to the Hatteras's appeal.

Hatteras visitors love the casual and laid-back style of the island. In the sun and the sand, in bathing suits and flip-flops, everyone is equal. The time of high tide matters, what one is wearing does not. Which direction the wind is going to blow tomorrow matters, how much money one makes does not. On Hatteras Island, residents and visitors live a stripped-down existence, in tune with the elements and the natural world, not the material world.

Hatteras Island visitors love the great outdoors. Those who are happiest here are those who love being close to nature. Anglers, windsurfers, kiteboarders, surfers, paddlers, swimmers, birders, beachcombers — these are the people who appreciate Hatteras Island the most. Hatteras Island vacationers love being outside all day then settling down for a great North Carolina seafood dinner at night. They love the fact that nightlife consists of an acoustic band at the local restaurant, a moonlit walk on the beach or going to bed early.

Visitors love the fact that there are only three stoplights on the entire island and that the main traffic artery is a two-lane road with many ocean and sound views. They love the locally owned businesses and the lack of homogenous superstores and chain restaurants. They love the locals, who are friendly and helpful as long as people are friendly and respectful to them.

In summer the villages swell to capacity, and there is a sense of excitement in the air. Locals stay busy — teaching kiteboarding lessons, leading kayak tours, waiting tables, cleaning rental cottages, booking hotel rooms, cutting fish down at the docks, answering questions about the lighthouse, giving directions. Many islanders do double duty in the summer, taking on more than one job to build a stockpile of money for the winter, when things slow down. The restaurants and shops are full and the grocery store lines are a nightmare. But it's all part of the fun of summer.

Many people say fall is the best time of year to visit Hatteras Island because the crowds are gone, the weather is still warm, all the businesses are open and accommodations prices drop. Anglers typically prefer fall to summer as fishing is far better in the autumn months. Winter is pretty quiet on Hatteras Island, but you'd be surprised how many accommodations and businesses are still open to serve locals and tourists. In the spring, visitors start to trickle back in. Businesses that have been closed all winter offer good deals to visitors who come early in the season.

Directions and Orientation

You can get to Hatteras Island by car, boat or small plane. The vast majority of visitors arrive by car from the north on N.C. Highway 12. Other car travelers arrive on the ferry from the southwest via Ocracoke Island. Some people arrive at Hatteras Island by boat from the mainland, the Intracoastal Waterway or the Atlantic Ocean. Marinas are available to boaters in Hatteras Village, at the southern end of the island by Hatteras Inlet. Flying to Hatteras Island is possible. Small planes can land at the National Park Service's Billy Mitchell Airfield in Frisco.

Once you get to the island, you will almost certainly need your own form of transportation. There is no public transportation on the island, and the villages are separated by long stretches of Cape Hatteras National Seashore. If you want to get from village to village you'll need a car. A bicycle is fine for getting around in the individual villages, though bicycling between the villages is not highly recommended because of the lack of a bike lane and the high speed of traffic.

On the north end of the island, about 12 miles from Oregon Inlet, are the three villages of **Rodanthe, Waves** and **Salvo,** which are all lumped together and feel more like one village than three. These are the simplest and most laid-back of the seven villages, though all the amenities anyone could need are there. Several miles south is the village of **Avon,** which feels like the commercial hub of the island because it has a major grocery store, movie theater, lots of stores and services, and numerous luxury rental homes. South of Avon is the village of **Buxton,** home of the Cape Hatteras Lighthouse, the prime surf-fishing grounds of the cape and the most hotels on the island. South of Buxton is **Frisco,** a very small, quiet village with lots of rental homes and a few shops and restaurants. **Hatteras Village,** on the south end of the island, leads a dual life now – partly a historic fishing village and partly an upscale vacation resort.

Those looking for the most watersports opportunities should stay in Rodanthe, Waves, Salvo or Avon. Those looking for the most peace and quiet should stay in Frisco, Waves or Salvo. Those who like to have a lot of restaurants and shops nearby should stay in Avon or Buxton. Serious anglers like staying in Hatteras Village, where all the marinas and offshore fishing boats are located.

If you're ready to start enjoying all that Hatteras Island has to offer, read on. The pages that follow are filled with all the hotels and motels, campgrounds, vacation rental companies, shops, restaurants, attractions and recreational opportunities on Hatteras Island. We have organized the businesses in this guide geographically from north to south, starting in Rodanthe and ending in Hatteras Village. Enjoy your stay! 𝒞

Hatteras Island Attractions ❧

The natural world is the most stunning attraction on the Outer Banks. It's hard for anything else to compete with the wonders that Mother Nature provides here, so many of the local points of interest are nature-oriented. But beyond the water, the landscape and the wildlife, there are some fantastic attractions that offer interesting diversions and inform visitors about the rich history of Hatteras Island. The island attractions are either free or charge a very modest fee. Several of the places listed here are also included on our Historic Tour, so you may want to reference back to that section for more information. Also see the Recreation section for other ways to get to know this island.

Pea Island National Wildlife Refuge

Hwy. 12, northern Hatteras Island
(252) 987-2394

The refuge's Visitor Center, located on the northern end of Hatteras Island about 4 miles south of Oregon Inlet, is a good place to start a Pea Island visit. It gives an introduction to the ecosystem and wildlife of the refugeand the activities that are permissible there. You can also pick up informational brochures and trail maps. A restroom and plenty of parking are available. You can start a hike around North Pond here (see the Hiking section of the Recreation chapter). Ask at the Visitor Center about the canoe tours and guided bird walks that are offered almost all year round or other programs that might be held during the summer. The Visitor Center is open 9 a.m. to 4 p.m. every day. Beyond the Visitor Center, Pea Island National Wildlife Refuge is a 13-mile stretch of pristine barrier island. The beaches are wonderfully devoid of people most of the time, and there are several access points for getting to the beach. Pea Island is also great for surfing, surf-fishing, shell-hunting, kayaking, photography and other eco-friendly outdoor activities. Driving on the beach is not allowed here.

Carl Bornfriend in the gift shop of the Frisco Native American Museum *knows more about Native American history on Hatteras Island than anyone around. Stop in and explore.*

Chicamacomico Life Saving Station

Hwy. 12, Rodanthe   (252) 987-1552

The Chicamacomico Life Saving Station is the most complete existing example of the life saving stations that were built along the coast in the late 19th century, the age of shipping, to attend to shipwrecks and rescue survivors. The 1874 station was one of the original life saving stations built along the Outer Banks, and it operated until 1954. (See site number 14 in the Historic Tour section for more information.) Chicamacomico has been restored, thanks to numerous volunteers who formed a nonprofit organization to save it, and it is now a fine museum and historic site. On a visit here

you'll see the 1874 Chicamacomico Life Saving Station (now a boat house for the surf boat), the 1911 Chicamacomico Life Saving Station, two cookhouses, a shop, a stable and a building that houses a collection of shipwreck artifacts. In the museum, you'll learn about the life saving service and some of the rescues that occurred here. The gift shop is full of unique nautical items and works by local craftsmen, plus books and old-fashioned toys. Try to catch any of the guided tours or programs offered from May through September. Call for a summer program schedule. The station is open from Easter weekend through Thanksgiving weekend, Monday through Friday from 9 a.m. to 5 p.m. Nominal admission is charged.

Cape Hatteras Lighthouse

Lighthouse Rd., Buxton

(252) 995-4474

If any one thing represents all of Hatteras Island, it has to be the famous black-and-white, spiral-striped Cape Hatteras Lighthouse. The lighthouse has become the icon of the island, representing the hopeful, stalwart, survivalist attitude that is so pervasive among the people of Hatteras.

This is perhaps the most famous lighthouses in the nation, especially since it survived a controversial, precarious move in 1999. Its rich history and importance to the island are detailed in our Historic Tour section, site 27. Now in the hands of the National Park Service, the Cape Hatteras Lighthouse is open to the public. Visitors 38 inches and taller can climb up to the top of the lighthouse for an unforgettable view of the Atlantic Ocean, Cape Hatteras and Buxton. The climb costs $6 for adults, $4 for children and seniors age 62 and older. The lighthouse is open from Easter weekend through Columbus Day, but be sure to call ahead for specific dates. Lighthouse tours begin at 9 a.m. daily and run every 20 minutes with a limit of 60 visitors per tour. The last tour of the day is at 4:40 p.m. This is a very popular attraction and no advance tickets are sold, so the best thing to do is to get there early (before noon) and visit the ticket booth to buy a ticket, which will state the time of your tour. Be sure to be at the gate five minutes before your tour time. A museum about lighthouses and the history of the Outer Banks is located inside the historic Double Keepers' Quarters Building just across the lawn from the lighthouse.

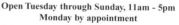

Hatteras Island Visitor Center

At the Cape Hatteras Lighthouse
Lighthouse Rd., Buxton

(252) 995-4474

The National Park Service's Hatteras Island Visitor Center is located at the Cape Hatteras Lighthouse site. Maps, informational brochures and the park newspaper are available here, and staff can answer any questions you have. Lots of parking and restrooms are on site. There's also a bookstore and gift shop. Inquire at the Visitor Center about the ranger-led history and nature programs that are held regularly from mid-June through mid-August. The Visitor Center is open 9 a.m. to 6 p.m. in the summer months and 9 a.m. to 5 p.m. the rest of the year.

Frisco Native American Museum & Natural History Center

Hwy. 12, Frisco   (252) 995-4440

The Native American history of Hatteras Island and the Native American culture of our nation are preserved at this must-see museum in Frisco. The owners, Joyce and Carl Bornfriend, have taken great care to preserve Native American heritage, and their collection of artifacts, exhibits and natural history displays is nationally recognized and respected. The galleries include information on Native Americans across the United States as well as arts and crafts from around the nation. Particularly interesting to Hatteras Island visitors are the artifacts from the Native Americans who once inhabited this island. Displays include a dugout canoe that was found on the property as well as tools, instruments and other items uncovered on the island in an archaeological dig sponsored by East Carolina University. The gift shop has a great variety of Native American-made items and arts and crafts, including books, walking sticks, dream-catchers, moccasins, jewelry, paintings, drums, pottery, handmade knives and much more. Friends of the Museum sponsor an antique room as a fund raiser for the museum. It is connected to the museum and offers an astonishing array of collectibles. While you're here, be sure to walk on the museum's nature trails that wind through several acres of maritime forest. The trails are open 24/7 and include displays on native wildlife, a mini-longhouse and special accommodations for visually impaired persons. Museum hours are 11 a.m. to 5 p.m. Tuesday through Sunday. Cost is $2 per person, $1.50 for seniors or $5 per family. Guided tours and special workshops/seminars for groups are available. The building that houses the museum is more than 100 years old; see site 34 on the Historic Tour for more information.

Blue Marlin Display

Hatteras Village Library and Community Center
Hwy. 12, Hatteras Village

Hatteras Village is the offshore fishing capital of the Outer Banks. Big-game marlin fishing began here in the 1930s. To see a blue marlin (one that's been mounted and preserved), go over to the Hatteras Village Library and Community Center. On the outside wall, encased in a glass box, is a world-record, 810-pound blue marlin that was caught on June 11, 1962, off Hatteras Island. The world record has since been broken, but this is still an impressive specimen.

Unloading Catches at the Docks

Hatteras Village Marinas, Hatteras Village

For a chance to see the offshore boats unloading the day's deep-sea catches, head down to one of the Hatteras Village marinas between 4 and 5 p.m. When the boats come in, the fishing mates unload the day's catches onto the docks so the fish can be taken away and cleaned. You'll see lots of tuna, mahi-mahi and wahoo plus some other interesting fish. The big game fish are caught and released, so you won't see all the white marlin, blue marlin and sailfish that were caught that day, though you can count the flags on the boats to see how many were released. If you're really lucky in the winter months you might see a boat bring in a giant bluefin tuna, a rare spectacle.

Graveyard of the Atlantic Museum

59200 Museum Dr. Hatteras Village
(252) 986-2996

At the end of N.C. Highway 12 next to the ferry terminal, the new Graveyard of the Atlantic Museum attracts a lot of attention in its unique, ship-like building with porthole windows and curved timbers holding up the roof. Though it is not yet fully complete due to lack of funds, the museum opened one exhibit, plus the gift shop, lobby and community room to the public in the summer of 2003. More than 60,000 visitors came to the museum to check it out. The new building is so beautiful inside and the opening exhibit on Brig. Gen. Billy Mitchell was so well done that it has built much excitement for what is to come when the museum raises the final $1.8 million it needs to complete its galleries and exhibits. When finished, the museum will focus on the maritime history and shipwrecks of North Carolina's Outer Banks, often called the Graveyard of the Atlantic. The mu-

seum will emphasize the periods from 1524 to 1945, with shipwreck artifacts and memorabilia on display and changing exhibits telling the dramatic tales of shipwrecks and lifesaving along the Carolina coast. For now, you can visit the museum for free and see the exhibit on maritime history and shipwrecks that's set up in the lobby area. If you like what you see, make a donation. This museum is destined to be a major attraction on the Carolina coast. When you're here, check out the historic markers in the parking lot, which tell interesting stories about war on the Outer Banks.

Hatteras-Ocracoke Ferry

End of Hwy. 12, Hatteras Village
(252) 986-235   (800) BY FERRY

For a free boat ride, drive onto the ferry at the south end of Hatteras Island. You'll cross Hatteras Inlet and end up on the absolutely charming island of Ocracoke, where you'll definitely want to spend a few hours or a whole day exploring the village shops, restaurants and historic sites (and pick up a copy of the sister book to this one on Ocracoke Island). The ferry ride is about 45 minutes long. Once you get off the ferry onto Ocracoke Island, you'll need transportation - your car or a bicycle - because it's about 13 miles from the ferry dock to the village. The ferry is free and it runs every 30 minutes in the summer season. 𝒆

Throughout the summer, the National Park Service offers a number of free programs for visitors. Look for their newspaper In The Park *for detailed schedules and information.*

Hatteras Island Recreation ❧

Hatteras Island is a Mecca for surfers, kiteboarders, windsurfers, anglers, birders, paddlers, campers, scuba divers and beach-lovers. The active and sporty crowd loves it here for a number of reasons — mild temperatures for about nine months of the year, abundant and accessible ocean and sound beaches, numerous outfitters catering to the various activities and the very laid-back lifestyle. Most important to Hatteras Island's outdoorsy personality, however, is Cape Hatteras National Seashore, a 72-mile park that includes parts of Bodie, Hatteras and Ocracoke islands and is left in its almost completely natural state. The National Seashore offers undeveloped ocean and sound beaches where eco-friendly outdoor recreation is encouraged and wildlife can be seen in its natural habitat. In the seven island villages, you'll find many outfitters offering all the gear, rentals and lessons you'll need to get out there and enjoy the great outdoors, barrier island style. The villages also offer other recreational opportunities, like mini-golf, movies and bike rentals.

The Beach

In North Carolina, all beach below the high-tide mark is public property. So you can enjoy any part of the beach as long as you get there legally. Public beach accesses are located along N.C. 12 throughout Cape Hatteras National Seashore and Pea Island National Wildlife Refuge, and there are numerous accesses in the villages. Do not access the beach via private property, i.e., cutting through private oceanfront yards to get there.

The only life-guarded beach on Hatteras Island is at the Cape Hatteras Lighthouse beach in the summer months. Otherwise, swimming is at your own risk. Many visitors are surprisingly unaware of the dangers of ocean swimming. Always regard the ocean with a sense of caution, no matter how good a swimmer you are. Rip currents, which suck objects and people from shore to sea, are the biggest threat swimmers may encounter. The most important thing to remember about rip currents is not to try to swim against them directly back to shore. Swim parallel to the beach to get out of the current, then swim diagonally into shore.

Educational materials about rip currents and other ocean dangers are available in local visitor centers. It's a good idea to carry some sort of flotation device with you when swimming, like a surfboard, body board or raft, but you can't totally depend on those for safety. Drownings have occurred when non-swimmers lost the rafts or body boards they were depending on for flotation. Another important thing about ocean swimming: Never take your eyes off your children, even if they're just wading in the surf. Children can be knocked down by waves and washed into the sea in the blink of an eye. We're not trying to discourage anyone from ocean swimming. Most days Atlantic Ocean swimming is safe and wonderful. Just be cautious and educated before going into the water.

If you're unsure about ocean swimming or if the day is particularly rough, you can also swim in the shallower, calmer waters of the Pamlico Sound. The sound is a good place for children and not-so-strong swimmers. It's a good idea to wear some kind of water shoes in the sound so you won't cut your feet on oyster shells. There are several soundside beaches within Cape Hatteras National Seashore. The most easily accessible are the Salvo Day Use area just south of Salvo and the Haulover area just south of Avon (see the Watersports section). Otherwise, if you have a four-wheel-drive vehicle, there are several sand trails in Cape Hatteras National Seashore that lead back to soundside beaches (see an Off-Road Driving Map, available at National Park Service Visitor Centers).

Note: For disabled visitors, Cape Hatteras National Seashore loans out beach wheelchairs on a first-come, first-served basis. For information call (252) 441-5711 or (252) 995-4474.

Beach Driving

Driving on the beach is allowed in some areas of Cape Hatteras National Seashore but not in the village boundaries or at Pea Island National Wildlife Refuge. If you want to go off-roading, pick up an Off-Road Driving Map at one of the National Seashore Visitors Centers at Bodie Island Lighthouse, Cape Hatteras Lighthouse or the campgrounds. You can access the beach by vehicle at one of several sand ramps along the island. Be sure to read any signage concerning beach driving; some areas are closed to driving during tourist season, bird-nesting season or if the beach has gotten too narrow to allow for safe driving. There are also several soundside off-road-vehicle trails listed on the maps. Driving on the ocean beach or the soundside trails can be very convenient, especially for anglers looking for the perfect spot to fish. It's also nice for families to be able to park a car next to the water and set up camp for the day.

Four-wheel-drive vehicles are an absolute necessity when driving in sand. You'll certainly be the subject of derisive snickering if you attempt it in a two-wheel-drive car and get stuck. But even four-wheel-drive vehicles get stuck from time to time. If you're going to attempt driving in sand, most people recommend lowering the air pressure in your tires to about 20 to 25 pounds to give the vehicle a little flotation on the sand. Try to follow in the tracks of vehicles that were there before you, and try to maintain a steady pace in the softer, deeper sand. If you do get stuck, a fellow off-roader will usually help you out. If not, call Cape Point Exxon Towing Service in Buxton at (252) 995-5695.

Bike Rentals

Biking is a good way to get around within the specific village you're staying in, but it's not the best way to see the entire island. The road between the villages (N.C. 12) is narrow with a very minimal bike lane and a 55 m.p.h. speed limit, so it's not really safe to cycle unless you're a professional. In the villages, however, the speed limit is slower though the road is really not very accommodating to bikers. Helmets are a good idea (in fact they're required in North Carolina for kids younger than 16), and kids should ride on side streets. If you want to rent a bicycle, here are a few options.

Just For The Beach
Waves   (252) 987-9939

Ocean Atlantic Rentals
Avon   (252) 995-5868

Island Cycles
Avon   (252) 995-4336

Lee Robinson's General Store
Hatteras Village   (252) 986-2381

Island Cycles
Hatteras Island Plaza, N.C. Hwy. 12,
Avon   (252) 995-4336
Serious cyclists will appreciate this full-service bike shop. They sell bikes and gear and make repairs when you need them. They also rent scooters and bikes for the whole family.

Boating

Getting out on the water is half the fun of being on Hatteras Island. If you've brought your own boat, we've listed the places to launch it below. If you'd like to rent a boat, check with Kinnakeet Adventures, (252) 995-3938. Boat launches will put you into the Pamlico Sound. If you're confident with your boat-handling skills and the weather and you want to boat in the ocean, you'll need to head through Oregon or Hatteras inlets.

Boat Launch Ramps
Oregon Inlet Fishing Center
North side of Oregon Inlet on Bodie Island, free launch and plenty of parking.
New Inlet Boat Ramp
Pea Island National Wildlife Refuge, free, small boats only
Salvo Market/Citgo
Salvo, fee per launch
Kinnakeet Adventures at The Avon Boathouse
Bonito Road, Avon, fee per launch
Frisco Cove Marina
Frisco, fee per launch
Teach's Lair Marina
Hatteras Village, fee per launch
Village Marina
Hatteras Village, fee per launch

Climbing Wall
Kitty Hawk Kites
Hatteras Landing, Marina Way,
Hatteras Village   (252) 986-1446
If all this flat land has you craving a vertical view of things, Kitty Hawk Kites has a sport rock-climbing wall set up on the porch at Hatteras Landing Marina. It

tops out at 32 feet high, and there are beginner and advanced routes. It's usually only open in the high season.

Fishing

Fishing is big business on Hatteras Island. The big-game fishing of the Gulf Stream is easily accessible from Hatteras Village marinas, and anglers head offshore for a chance to fight blue and white marlin, sailfish and giant bluefin tuna or to bring in a healthy catch of yellowfin tuna and mahi-mahi. Anyone can charter a boat to take them offshore fishing. The boats take up to six passengers and supply all the bait and tackle you'll need, plus a mate who'll do everything but reel in your fish.

Fishing in the sound, on near-shore wrecks, in the surf and from piers is equally popular. During certain times of the year, especially fall and spring, surf fishing is phenomenal on Hatteras Island. Red drum, striped bass and blue fish are some of the favorite fall surf catches, along with flounder, trout, sea mullet and pompano in the summer. If you need a little surf-fishing advice, ask at the local tackle shops. Numerous guides are available to take you out on inshore fishing trips in the sound or on near-shore ocean wrecks. There are currently three fishing piers on Hatteras Island.

Tackle Shops

Finding fishing bait, tackle and gear is never a problem on Hatteras Island. There may seem to be a disproportionate number of tackle shops on the island, but fishing is so good here they all stay busy.

Mac's Tackle-Island Convenience
Rodanthe (252) 987-2239
Hatteras Jack
Rodanthe (252) 987-2428
JoBob's Trading Post
Rodanthe (252) 987-2201
The Fishing Hole
Salvo (252) 987-2351
Frank and Fran's
Avon (252) 995-4171
Dillon's Corner
Buxton (252) 995-5083
The Red Drum
Buxton (252) 995-5414
Lighthouse Tackle
Buxton (252) 995-3000
Frisco Tackle
Frisco (252) 995-4361
Frisco Rod and Gun
Frisco (252) 995-5366
Angler's Headquarters
Hatteras Village (252) 986-2989
Oden's Dock
Hatteras Village (252) 986-2555
Teach's Lair Marina
Hatteras Village (252) 986-2460

Fishing Charters

If you're looking for an inshore charter, ask at the local tackle shops or call the Hatteras Village marinas; most of them recommend inshore guides. If you're looking for an offshore charter, refer to the list below.

Hatteras Watersports (252) 987-2306
Soundside Charters (252) 995-4114
Got 'Em Inshore Charters
(252) 995-3707 (252)987-3143
Hatteras Light Tackle Fishing Trips
(252) 995-4679
Oden's Dock (252) 986-2555

The Albatross Fleet of Hatteras
North Carolina's Pioneer Charter Fishing Fleet

Gulfstream and Inshore Fishing since 1937

(252) 986-2515

Albatross Fleet Foster's Quay
(252) 986-2515
Village Marina (252) 986-2522
Hatteras Harbor Marina
(252) 986-2166
Hatteras Landing Marina
(252) 986-2077

Albatross Fleet / Foster's Quay

Hatteras Village (252) 986-2515

Foster's Quay, on the harbor in Hatteras Village, is the docking site of the Albatross Fleet fishing charters. Captain Ernie Foster, a second-generation Hatteras fishing guide, operates three sister charter vessels — *Albatross I, II* and *III* — from these docks. These unique, round-sterned boats were designed specifically for fishing in Hatteras waters and they began the charter-fishing industry in Hatteras in 1937. Foster offers offshore trips, inshore trips and winter bluefin tuna trips.

Fishing Head Boat

Miss Hatteras

Oden's Dock, Hwy. 12, Hatteras
(252) 986-2365

This 75-foot head boat makes daily trips to the fishing grounds, with individuals paying "by the head" to go along. All the gear and tackle you'll need is provided. The Miss Hatteras takes full-day trips to the Gulf Stream and half-day trips to wrecks to bottom fish for bluefish, trout, sea bass, flounder and more. Reservations are required. Call for prices and times. Also at Oden's Dock is the Little Clam, a 42-foot boat that makes inshore and nearshore fishing trips for Spanish and king mackerel and other fish.

See **www.hatterasguide.com** for full content, links & updates.

Fishing Piers

Hatteras Island Resort Fishing Pier

24251 Atlantic Ave., Rodanthe
(252) 987-2323

This fishing pier, locally called the Rodanthe Pier, offers some of the best fishing on Hatteras Island. Daily, weekly and seasonal passes are available, and the pier is open from April through January 2. The pier house offers bait, tackle sales and rentals, snacks, drinks, beach supplies, souvenirs, restrooms and a game room.

Avon Fishing Pier

Hwy. 12, Avon   (252)995-5480

Stretching about 600 feet into the Atlantic Ocean, Avon Pier offers excellent fishing plus a pier house store selling fishing gear, bait and tackle, drinks, sandwiches, gifts and T-shirts. You can also rent fishing gear if you need it. All-day fishing passes cost $8 for adults, $6 for seniors and $5 children. Sightseers are charged $1. The pier is open from 6 a.m. until midnight, but in October and November, when drum fishing is hot, it stays open 24 hours. Ask about the October drum tournament and the August children's tournament. The Avon Pier closes in the winter months.

Cape Hatteras Fishing Pier (Frisco Pier)

Cape Hatteras Pier Dr.,
off Hwy 12, Frisco   (252) 986-2533

The Cape Hatteras Fishing Pier, called the Frisco Pier, is a very popular fishing spot. They offer snacks, drinks, bait and tackle and other supplies fishermen need.

If you need something to make your vacation more fun, it can be rented on Hatteras.

See **www.hatterasguide.com** for full content, links & updates.

Party Boat Fishing!
on
MISS HATTERAS

Full Day Offshore
Sea Bass · Snapper · Trigger · Grouper
Wed, Fri, Sat & Sun · 6:30 am-4:30 pm

1/2 Day Inshore Fishing
Trout · Croakers · Flounder & Bluefish
Tues & Thurs · 8:00 am-Noon
Call for info about our Fall King Mackerel trips

Fast 75' Boat

MISS HATTERAS

Dolphin Watching Cruises
Thurday · 6:00-7:30 pm

Docked At Oden's Dock, Hatteras Village . (252) 986-2365

Party Boat Fishing
on
MISS HATTERAS

Full Day Offshore
Sea Bass · Snapper · Trigger · Grouper
Wed, Fri, Sat & Sun · 6:30 am-4:30 pm

1/2 Day Inshore Fishing
Trout · Croakers · Flounder & Bluefish
Tues & Thurs · 8:00 am-Noon
Call for info about our Fall King Mackerel trips

Fast 75' Boat

Dolphin Watching Cruises
Thurday · 6:00-7:30 pm

Docked At Oden's Dock, Hatteras Village . (252) 986-236

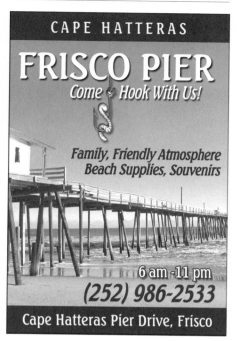
Marinas

The island marinas are the hubs of the fishing community. The fishing boats dock here, and the catches are unloaded here at the end of the day. Most of the marinas rent slips with full hookups to transient and resident boaters.

Frisco Cove Marina

Frisco (252) 995-4242

Frisco Cove Marina offers slip rentals, gas and a boat ramp. It costs $10 to use the boat ramp, but parking is limited.

Oden's Dock

Hatteras Village (252) 986-2555

Oden's Dock books inshore and offshore fishing charters year round, in addition to duck hunting charters in the winter months. A couple of headboats operate from here. Slip rentals with electric and water hookups are available. Oden's sells gas and diesel fuel, and the Ship's Store sells tackle, oil, food, drinks and gift items. Rod and reel repairs are done here.

Foster's Quay

Hatteras Village (252) 986-2515

Foster's Quay is the docking site of the Albatross fleet fishing charters. It's right between Oden's and Village Marina.

Village Marina & Campground

Hatteras Village (252) 986-2522

The folks at Village Marina call this the "best dinky marina anywhere." Small it is, yet Village offers slip rentals with water and electric hookups, a boat ramp, gas and a ship's store. See the Accommodations chapter for more about the

campground. Look for a new motel and a new restaurant here.

Hatteras Harbor Marina
Hatteras Village   (252) 986-2166

This full-service marina books offshore and inshore fishing trips year round with a 20-boat charter fleet. They offer deepwater slip rentals with water and electric hookups and sell diesel fuel. Shower and laundry facilities, apartment rentals, a ship's store and a deli are on site.

Teach's Lair Marina
Hatteras Village   (252) 986-2460

Teach's Lair is a full-service marina offering both inshore and offshore fishing charters year round. Slip rentals with hookups are available by the day, week, month or year. A ramp for launching boats can be used for a fee. A conve-

nience store, ship's store and tackle shop are onsite, as is a new restaurant, Teach's Island Bar and Grill. Gas and diesel fuel are sold here.

Hatteras Landing Marina
Hatteras Village   (252) 986-2077

The southernmost marina on the island, next to the ferry docks, books both inshore and offshore fishing charters year round, including make-up charters for only $175 per person. Slip rentals for boats up to 75 feet are available, with power and water hookups at every slip. Showers, laundry facilities, a well-stocked ship's store, several shops, a bakery, a deli and a world-class restaurant are on site here.

Fitness and Spa

Island Fitness Club

Light Plant Rd., Buxton
(252) 995-5339
Across from Conner's Supermarket, this fitness center features cardiovascular and weight-training equipment. Yearly, monthly, weekly and daily passes are available. It's open every day.

Spa Koru

Hwy. 12, Avon   (252) 995-3125
Opening in spring 2005, Spa Koru is the most upscale, chi chi thing ever to happen to Hatteras Island. With a beautiful South Pacific theme and interior, it features a full menu of spa treatments, including massage and skin and body care. The spa also has a hair and nail salon and a retail boutique. The complete fitness center features top of the line equipment, and there are group exercise classes, including yoga, available with a membership or on a drop-in basis. It's located in Avon next to the Medical Center.

In Touch Massage and Wellness Center

Hwy. 12, Frisco   (252) 995-4067
In Touch Massage and Wellness Center offers a haven of peace and restoration on Hatteras Island. Only organic products are used in the massage therapy and spa treatments. Pamper yourself with treatments such as a brown-sugar scrub or herbal-salt scrub combined with a massage, or choose a mud wrap or a facial. There are four treatment rooms and group appointments are available. An acupuncturist, chiropractor and counselors also offer services here. The center

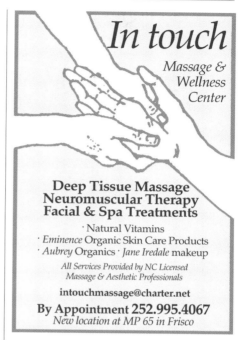

sells organic skin-care products, yoga and Pilates equipment, homeopathic treatments and other wellness products. Ask about the meditation classes and personal-growth workshops. In Touch is located in the same building as Indiantown Gallery and Island Perks Coffee Shop, so be sure to visit all three.

Flying/Air Tours

Burrus Flying Service

Billy Mitchell Airport, Frisco
(252) 986-2679
For a totally different perspective on Hatteras Island, see it from the air. Burrus offers air tours over Hatteras and Ocracoke islands for sightseeing, aerial photography or historical tours. Custom tours are available. Air tours range from $75 to $135.

Game Rooms

Froggy Dog

Hwy. 12, Avon   (252) 995-4106

The Froggy Dog's game room has four pool tables, pinball, darts and a great arcade. There's also a "Tadpole Corner" for kids.

Mack Daddy's Crab Shack

Hwy. 12, Avon   (252) 995-5060

Mack Daddy's Game Room has a pool table, darts and video games. It's open during restaurant hours, at dinner only.

Angelo's Pizza

Hwy. 12, Buxton   (252) 995-6900

The game room at this restaurant is enormous, great for kids who are looking for something to do. There are several pool tables, foosball tables, air hockey and tons of video games, plus a snack bar with candy and soft drinks. Call for hours.

Frisco Mini-Golf and Go-Karts

Hwy. 12, Frisco   (252) 995-6325

The game room at Frisco Mini-Golf has pool tables, air hockey, video games and snacks like ice cream, nachos and hot dogs and drinks. It's open seven days a week, as are the golf course and go-kart tracks.

Golf

Avon Golf

Avon Fishing Pier, 41001 Hwy. 12
Avon   (252) 995-5480

To practice your putting skills, head over to Avon Golf. This 18-hole, natural-grass putting green is miraculously lush, considering its oceanfront location. Unlimited, all-day play costs $8, and you can come and go as you please. The course is open from 11 a.m. until midnight. Get your tickets at the Avon Fishing Pier.

Uncle Eddy's Frozen Custard and 18-Hole Minigolf

Hwy. 12, Buxton   (252) 995-4059

Next to Falcon Motel, this is the place for summer fun. The 18-hole mini-golf course is nestled under live oaks, providing a shady spot to get out of the sun. Unlimited play costs $5 for adults and $2 for kids. After golf, cool down with the delicious homemade frozen custard this place is known for. There are more than 50 homemade flavors, from the fruity Hatteras Sunrise to Rum Raisin.

Frisco Mini-Golf and Go-Karts
Hwy. 12, Frisco   (252) 995-6325

For a day or night of good, clean fun, head 1.5 miles south of Buxton to this Frisco recreational facility. The mini-golf course has 18 holes in a natural setting with waterfalls and fish ponds. You can play all day until 5 p.m. for one fee. After 5 p.m., there is a charge per a round of golf. There are two go-kart tracks here — a slick track and a family track. Drivers must be at least 54 inches tall, but little kids can ride with an adult. There's also a game room here. Everything is open from 11 a.m. to 11 p.m. seven days a week in season. There's plenty of parking for larger vehicles like RVs.

Ocean Edge Golf Course
Hwy. 12, Frisco   (252) 995-4100

If you just can't bear to leave your golf game behind when you're on vacation, be sure to visit this nine-hole executive golf course. Play it twice and you'll get in 18 holes. It's open year round, and you'll need to reserve a tee time in summer. Rates are reasonable ($30 for 18 holes; $20 for nine), and carts are included. It's open seven days a week year round.

Hiking
Pea Island National Wildlife Refuge
Hwy. 12, northern Hatteras Island
(252) 987-2394

A good, flat, easy hike starts at the Pea Island Visitor Center, about 4 miles south of Oregon Inlet. Park in the parking lot and look for the North Pond trailhead behind the restrooms. A sturdy, handi-capped-accessible boardwalk leads back into the marshy areas around North Pond, where you'll see a variety of birds and wildlife. After the boardwalk ends, you can keep going on an unpaved service road that takes you all the way around the pond. The North Pond Trail connects with the Salt Flats Trail, and at the end (N.C. 12) you can either turn back and go the way you came or walk down N.C. 12 or along the beach to get back to the Visitor Center. The entire loop, if you take the beach route, is about four miles. You can also park at the Salt Flats trailhead, a little over a mile north of the Visitor Center. You'll see a lot of birds on these trails no matter what time of year you're here, but this hike is most phe-nomenal in the fall and winter, when thousands of migratory birds are resting over on the pond. You'll see snow geese, Canada geese, tundra swan and numerous species of ducks. You can pick up trail maps at the Visitor Center from 9 a.m. to 4 p.m. every day. Ask about the guided bird walks held here.

Buxton Woods Coastal Reserve
Off Hwy. 12, Buxton and south
(252) 261-8891
Contact: N.C. Division of Coastal Management

Buxton Woods is the largest remain-ing maritime forest in the Southeast. It consists of pine- and oak-covered dune ridges interspersed with maritime swamp forest and unique marshy wetlands. It's a very rare ecosystem for a barrier island, and most visitors don't even realize it exists. The N.C. Division of Coastal Management maintains a 968-acre portion of the woods for research, education and recreation and offers some great hiking trails for the public to use to experience this amazing ecosystem. On a walk here you might see one of 360 species of birds, including bald eagles and peregrine falcons, plus gray fox, white-tailed deer, mink, river otter, box turtles, salamanders or other creatures.

A great hiking trail can be found just south of Buxton. Off N.C. 12, turn east onto Old Doctor's Road. If you have a four-wheel-drive vehicle, keep heading straight back on that sand road until it dead ends. If you don't have four-wheel-drive, park your car on the little turnout off to the side of Old Doctor's Road. At the end of the sand road is a trailhead sign for a one-third mile hike that takes you up to a high dune ridge. From this ridge you can look down at Jennette's Sedge, a beautiful interdunal pond teeming with life. If you walk from the beginning of the road to the trail and back, it will take you about an hour.

Another trail through Buxton Woods is a little south of the one on Old Doctor's Road. Turn east on Water Association Road and take the road all the way back until you reach a 90-degree bend in the road. At the corner of Water Association Road and Great Ridge Road, you'll find the trailhead. Park there. If you take a right, you'll follow a big, two-mile loop through the woods and back around to your car at Great Ridge Road. If you take a left, you'll go through forest and over dunes to the beach. You'll need to be able to walk in deep sand and over fallen trees and the like. Then you'll turn around come back the way you came, and the entire walk will have been about 3 miles.

The Coastal Reserve staff recently set up two kiosks to make these trails more user-friendly. Both contain hiking trail maps. One is on Old Doctor's Road and the other is down Water Association Road.

Buxton Woods – National Park Service Nature Trail
Lighthouse Rd.,Buxton (252) 995-4474

Near the lighthouse on the NPS grounds is a three-quarter-mile trail through the maritime forest of Buxton Woods. When heading toward the lighthouse, turn right on the road that heads toward the Cape Point Campground. The trailhead is at the picnic area. A pine-needle-covered path leads back into the forest. Along the way there are informational signs about the maritime forest ecosystem and the health of Buxton Woods. You'll pass Jennette's Sedge, a naturally occurring freshwater pond. This is a mostly flat, easy walk, though it's not recommended for the disabled because of slightly rough terrain.

Historical Tours

Hatteras Tours
(252) 475-4477

For an historian's perspective of Hatteras Island, you won't want to miss this bus tour of Hatteras Island. Island native Danny Couch leads tours in a 25-passenger mini-bus, telling fascinating stories and bits of island history along the way. Couch grew up on the island and is passionate about its history. The stories he tells will intrigue you. On Mondays at 10 a.m. he gives the Chicamacomico Tour, starting at Camp Hatteras. On Tuesdays at 8:45 a.m. he gives the Ocracoke Tour, starting at the Graveyard of the Atlantic Museum. Thursdays and Fridays there are two tours: 10 a.m. Kinnakeet to Buxton, starting at Hatteras Realty in Avon, and 2 p.m. Hatteras to Buxton, starting at the Museum. On Wednesdays you can take a

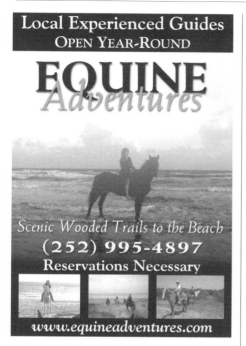

tour of Roanoke Island, starting at 8:45 a.m. Call for pickup. Ticket prices range from $25 to $45, depending on the season and the tour. Call the number above for more information or to reserve your seat.

Horseback Riding

Equine Adventures
Piney Ridge Rd., Frisco
(252) 995-4897

Equine Adventures offers two-hour guided horseback rides through the scenic trails of Frisco Woods and on the beach. All levels of riders are accommodated, but children younger than 12 or people weighing more than 225 pounds are not accepted. Rides are offered year round. You must make reservations in advance. Rides cost $80 per person.

Movies

Avon Movies 4
Hatteras Island Plaza, Hwy. 12
Avon   (252) 995-9060

Avon Movies offers four first-run movies daily. Beware of rainy days, when the theater is most crowded —advance tickets are available. For movie info, check The Island Breeze or call the hotline at the number above.

Village Video
Avon   (252) 995-5138
Buxton   (252) 995-6227
Rodanthe   (252) 987-2988
Hatteras   (252) 986-2181

For those rainy days and mellow nights, Village Video rents movies of every genre for every age group. They

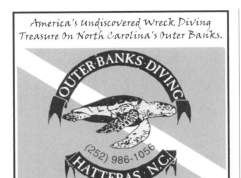
Diamond Shoals Band and other local musicians, poetry readings and storytelling. The music is bluegrass and folk, and everyone – performers and spectators alike – has a great time. The regular shows run Thursday nights from 8 to 10 p.m. Call for prices.

Scuba Diving

Outer Banks Diving
Hwy. 12, Hatteras Village
(252) 986-1056

For expert guiding and charters to the Graveyard of the Atlantic wrecks, certified divers should contact Outer Banks Diving. This full-service dive shop offers single, group and multi-day rates for trips on the *Bayou Runner* and *Dolphin* with Capt. Johnny and Amy Pieno. Wrecks are predominantly of WWII vintage in the 70- to 110-foot range. The boat is docked at Teach's Lair Marina, and the shop is about a mile north of there. The shop also offers rentals and repairs and sells gear, wetsuits and more. The gift shop is really neat, with giant sharks' teeth and souvenirs.

have the best selection of new releases in Hatteras. VHS and DVD movie rentals are available. Vacationers are welcome, and no membership is required. They also rent PlayStation II.

Music

Local restaurants often have acoustic music or bands in the summer, and the Frisco Jubilee promises regularly scheduled performances.

Frisco Jubilee
Red Drum Pottery Theater,
Hwy. 12, Frisco   (252) 995-5757

From June through September and occasionally on holiday weekends, the folks at Red Drum Pottery open their theater for the fun-filled Frisco Jubilee. It's an Opry-style show featuring the

Watersports
Surfing, Kiteboarding, Windsurfing, Paddling, Sailing

Hatteras Island is heaven for watersports enthusiasts. Surfers discovered the legendary waves of the Hatteras Island beaches more than four decades ago, and they're still coming in droves. When a tropical storm approaches from the south in late summer or fall, surfers from all along the East Coast get to Hatteras Island however they can. Surfboard

Kayaking is as fun in the ocean as it is in the sound.

rentals and sales and surfing lessons are offered here.

Windsurfers and kiteboarders alike appreciate the shallow waters of the Pamlico Sound around Hatteras Island. They also like the nearly constant wind of the Outer Banks, the easy sound access that Cape Hatteras National Seashore provides, and the lack of obstructions, like power lines and bridges, over the sound waters. In fact, those on the kiteboarding scene generally agree that Hatteras Island is the best place in the world for the sport, for novices and professionals alike. So, as you can imagine, kiteboarding is extremely popular here. There are several kiteboarding schools and camps on the island to teach people this relatively new sport. Instruction has improved greatly over the last couple of years, and thousands of people are learning the sport here each summer.

Because it is potentially dangerous for the untrained, kiteboarding equipment is not rented. You can take lessons or buy your own gear. Windsurfing lessons, rentals and sales are offered at many outfitters on the island.

Paddlers love the waters of Pamlico Sound. Kayak and canoe rentals are offered at many places, and some outfitters offer kayak eco-tours for all levels of paddlers. Experienced paddlers will get a thrill from riding the ocean waves. Sailors can also enjoy a day on the Pamlico Sound, but remember that the near-shore waters are not at all deep, so a small, shallow-draft boat is essential.

Keep in mind that personal water-craft, like Jet-Skis and Waverunners, are illegal to launch or land within the boundaries of Cape Hatteras National Seashore. You can launch or land within the village boundaries, but not from anywhere else. Otherwise, watersports

See **www.hatterasguide.com** for full content, links & updates.

Windsurfers travel from all around the world to challenge the waves and wind of Hatteras.

launching is allowed anywhere that's not private property. Many outfitters are located on the soundside of the island, so you can launch any gear you rent from them right on site. Cape Hatteras National Seashore offers unlimited access on the ocean and several soundside access roads that make it easy to get on the sound. As with the rest of this book, we present the information on watersports spots and shops from north to south, beginning in Rodanthe and ending in Hatteras Village.

Salvo Day Use area
Hwy. 12 south of Salvo

This is a very cool spot for hanging out by the sound. The site is a former National Park Service Campground that was closed due to lack of funds. The former campground area is a little unkempt and overgrown, but the roads and soundside beach are kept up nicely. When you turn in, head to the right to the northwest corner of the lot. There you'll find a parking area

next to a small cemetery. The sound beach is an awesome spot for fishing, launching a kite board, sail board or kayak, swimming or sitting in the sun. It's usually not very crowded, and the calm water is great for kids when the ocean is rough. Be sure to walk through the little cemetery before you leave. Some of the oldest island names are on the headstones, the oldest of which dates to 1872.

Haulover Day Use Area
Hwy. 12 south of Avon

The Haulover Day Use Area is also known as Canadian Hole because it is a hotspot for windsurfers, many of whom hail from Canada. This soundside access makes a day on the sound very convenient. There's lots of parking plus a bathhouse with rinse-off showers, changing rooms and restrooms. This little beach can be quite the scene when it's packed with windsurfers and kiteboarders, but a lot of families come here, too, to swim, kayak and sit on the beach.

Rodanthe Surf Shop
Hwy. 12, Rodanthe

(252) 987-2412

Rodanthe Surf Shop exists for the love of surfing alone. They rent body, surf and skim boards, and this is the place to custom order your own Hatteras Glass Surfboard, shaped on site.

Rodanthe Watersports and Campground
Hwy. 12, Rodanthe

(252) 987-1431

Rodanthe Watersports offers rentals of Waverunners, kayaks, sailboats, surf boards, skim boards, body boards, wetsuits, beach chairs and umbrellas. Right on the sound, it offers easy, uncrowded access to the water. Look for this business next to Lisa's Pizzeria.

Hatteras Island Sail Shop
Hwy. 12, Waves   (252) 987-2292

This soundfront recreation center offers rentals of kayaks, sailboats and windsurfing equipment plus lessons in windsurfing and kiteboarding. An onsite launching facility makes it easy to slip into the water. Kayak eco-tours are offered here, and the staff specializes in teaching watersports to children.

Hatteras Island Surf Shop
Hwy. 12, Waves   (252) 987-2296

This classic surf shop in an old cottage has been a fixture on the island surf scene for more than 30 years. The shop sells new and used boards and surf-related gear and rents surf, body and skim boards plus beach gear. Surf lessons are available.

See **www.hatterasguide.com** for full content, links & updates.

Windsurfing Hatteras is more than just a retail store, it's a complete watersports center located right on Pamlico Sound!

- Knowledgeable People
- Great Instruction
- Killer Selection

www.windsurfinghatteras.com
252.995.5000
866.995.6644

Kitty Hawk Kites

St. Waves Plaza, Hwy. 12, Waves
(252) 987-1100   (877) FLY-THIS;
Camp Hatteras   (252) 984-1044

Kitty Hawk Kites offers both ocean and sound kayak rentals at the Waves location, as well as at Camp Hatteras. For information or to make reservations call (877) FLY-THIS.

REAL Kiteboarding
Lesson Center

Hwy. 12, Waves
(252) 987-9990   (866) REAL-KITE

You can't miss REAL Kiteboarding's compound of red buildings in the heart of Waves. This is the REAL Lesson Center, right on the Pamlico Sound, and a perfect place for learning the sport. REAL Kiteboarding invented the Kite

Camp in 2000, and they've taken kiteboarding instruction to world-renowned levels since then. REAL's most popular lesson package is a three-day camp called "Zero to Hero" that promises results, but there are numerous other kiteboarding lessons offered, including half- and full-day programs. Watch kiteboarders rip across the sound while you catch up on some work or email. Ask about the accommodations and high-speed wireless Internet access.

Hatteras Watersports

Hwy. 12, Salvo   (252) 987-2306

Hatteras Watersports rents Wave Runners and Jet Skis for launching in the sound right on site. They also rent kayaks, which you can launch here or take to your own location. Beach Cruisers are available for rent as well. Between your adventures on the water, this is a great place to hang out, with a big lawn, sound beach, volleyball court, picnic area and restrooms with hot showers. Look for the big old house on the huge lot on the water. The house is actually the former Pea Island Coast Guard Station.

Kitty Hawk Kites

Island Shops, Hwy. 12, Avon
(252) 995-6060   (877) FLY-THIS

Kitty Hawk Kites offers both ocean and sound kayak rentals at its Avon store. You can launch at this site or take the kayak to your own location. Kitty Hawk Kites offers a variety of kayak eco-tours, including a great tour at Pea Island. They also offer kiteboarding lessons at various places along the Outer Banks. For information or to make reservations, call (877) FLY-THIS.

Windsurfing Hatteras

Hwy. 12, Avon   (252) 995-5000

Windsurfing Hatteras is watersports central. It's a full-service center offering windsurfing lessons, rentals and gear for sale. They also specialize in kiteboarding, with gear for sale and expert instruction, including group camps and private lessons offered by people who truly know the sport and know how best to teach it to others. Windsurfing Hatteras also rents kayaks, Waverunners and catamarans. This center is right on the sound, and you can launch from their dock. The store sells clothing, wetsuits, sandals and sunglasses and gear from Naish and North Sails.

Sail World

Dairy Queen Shopping Center,
Hwy. 12, Avon   (252) 995-5441

Sail World is a full-service windsurfing shop, offering rentals, lessons and gear. They also offer kiteboarding lessons and gear. The store sells backpacks, streetwear, swimwear, wetsuits, sunglasses and pretty much anything else the active crowd needs.

Ocean Atlantic Rentals

Hwy. 12, Avon   (252) 995-5868

Ocean Atlantic Rentals rents surf boards, body boards, skim boards, wetsuits, fins, kayaks and kayaking accessories. You can rent by the day or week. OAR will deliver to your cottage.

Hatteras Island Boardsports

Hwy. 12, Avon   (252) 995-6160

Hatteras Island Boardsports rents kayaks, windsurfers, surfboards, body boards, skim boards, bikes, beach gear and wetsuits and delivers your gear for free. You can also take group or private surfing lessons or participate in a guided kayak tour.

Ride Hatteras

Hwy. 12, Avon   (252) 995-6755

Ride Hatteras offers windsurfing and kiteboarding lessons for beginner, intermediate or advanced riders. Equipment is tailored to meet the needs of the student and the wind conditions of the day. Kids' lessons are available, and class sizes are small. They also offer surfing lessons for all ages. Kiteboarding lessons are popular here as are the surfing lessons for all ages. You can rent equipment for kiteboarding and surfing here, and they sell other essential gear.

Kinnakeet Adventures at The Avon Boathouse

Bonito Rd., Avon   (252) 995-3938

Kinnakeet Adventures, on the sound in Avon, offers a boat ramp, boat slips in a quiet marina, a dock for fishing and crabbing, and plenty of opportunities to get you on the water. Kayak tours are offered here, including sunset tours, all-ages family tours, special full-moon tours, kayak fishing tours and more. They also rent kayaks, paddle boats, motorized canoes, sailboats (Hobie Cats) and motor boats. They deliver rental boats for free, or you can launch from the site.

Fox Watersports

Hwy. 12, Buxton   (252) 995-4372

Fox specializes in windsurfing,

kiteboarding and surfing. You can buy all the gear you'll need for these sports plus get lessons and rentals for wind-surfing and surfing and lessons in kite- boarding. You can also rent surfboards, kayaks, body boards and skim boards and purchase sunglasses, clothes, flip flops or a wetsuit.

REAL Kiteboarding

Bilbo's Plaza, N.C. Hwy. 12, Buxton
(252) 995-4740   (866) REAL-KITE

REAL Kiteboarding, the industry leader in kiteboarding camps and lessons, has its headquarters in Buxton. Call or stop in to sign up for the camps, which guarantee that you'll be kiting within three days. The camps cover everything the student needs to know, and the atmosphere is relaxed and fun. Numerous lesson packages are offered. REAL has tons of gear and accessories for sale. This store also offers high-speed wireless Internet access for visitors.

Kitty Hawk Kites

Hatteras Landing, Marina Way,
Hatteras Village
(252) 986-1446   (877) FLY-THIS

Kitty Hawk Kites offers both ocean and sound kayak rentals and kayak eco-tours, including a great tour at Pea Island and at Hatteras Landing. They also offer kiteboarding lessons at various places along the Outer Banks. For information or to make reservations, call (877) FLY-THIS. 🦢

Hatteras Island Shopping ❧

Hatteras Island is not what one would expect as a shopping destination. Nonetheless, there are wonder-ful stores here, and if you want to do some browsing and shopping on Hatteras, you'll be pleased with the quality and variety of opportunities. The shops on the island are all locally owned, which allows for great individual character, and the staff members are always friendly & helpful.

If you're out looking for something fun, you'll happen upon it. Souvenirs abound, from miniature lighthouses to design-your-own T-shirts to local artwork. You'll also find clothes, bathing suits, beach toys, watersports equipment, home decor, gourmet food and incredible artwork by local and national artists. You could easily spend an entire day cruising among the island's shops from Rodanthe to Hatteras Village, though the biggest concentrations of retail stores are in Avon, Buxton and Hatteras Village.

If you're looking for necessities, you'll find what you need, whether it's a get-well card, a good book for the beach, a latch for the screen door or backing for your fly line. One chain grocery store and a couple of smaller, charming mom-and-pop grocers fill the food needs on the island. You'll find tackle stores in every village, and watersports equipment shops everywhere.

Rodanthe, Waves & Salvo

Austin's South Island Seafood and Produce
Hwy. 12, Rodanthe   (252) 987-1352

The name says it all. This market is the place to get fresh seafood and fresh produce when you want to do your own cooking. The Austin family is a trusted name in the Outer Banks seafood business.

Island Convenience Store
23532 Hwy. 12,
Rodanthe   (252) 987-2239

Island Convenience is a one-stop shop. They sell gas, groceries, beer and wine, beach supplies, gas, film, sundries, ice, souvenirs, film, T-shirts and other clothing, plus they have a bait and tackle

shop and a deli for quick meals (see Marilyn's Deli in Restaurants).

Rodanthe Surf Shop
23580 Hwy. 12,
Rodanthe   (252) 987-2412
This classic, surf-only shop has been a Rodanthe fixture for more than 15 years. Rodanthe Surf Shop is the real thing – a hardcore surf shop with no fluff or over-commercialized merchandise. This is the place to get your own Hatteras Glass Surfboard, which are shaped on site by custom order only. There's also clothing for men, women and children, plus sunglasses and other surf-related needs. It's in the little house next to the Texaco station.

Sea Chest
Hwy. 12, Rodanthe (252) 987-2303
Sea Chest's name is right on target. This store is a veritable treasure chest offering an incredible assortment of stuff – hermit crabs, chimes, kites, stained glass, figurines, books, calendars, jewelry, carvings, nautical souvenirs, collectibles and so much more we couldn't possibly name it all here. The back of the store is dedicated to antiques, with lots of china, dishes, and collectibles.

Hotline Thrift Shops
Hwy. 12, Rodanthe   (252) 473-5121
This thrift shop raises funds for Hotline, a crisis shelter and domestic violence prevention service for women and children. You can donate used items or buy goods at reasonable prices. For information about hours, call the main office in Manteo at (252) 473-5121. Look for it in a gray building in front of Rodanthe Fire Station.

North Beach Campground Store
Hwy. 12, Rodanthe   (252) 987-2378
This gas station offers groceries, drinks and snacks, fireworks, RV supplies and some tackle. It's also the headquarters for the North Beach Campground.

Hatteras Jack
Hwy. 12, Rodanthe   (252) 987-2428
Hatteras Jack is well-known for its expertise in building custom rods and reels. They also offer expert repairs of fishing equipment. They stock all the bait and tackle you could need for a Hatteras Island Fishing trip, and they can hook you up with a fishing charter. Ice and drinks are available, and this is a weigh station.

JoBob's Trading Post

N.C. Hwy. 12   (252) 987-2201

Fresh seafood is the main thing at JoBob's. Fresh clams, oysters, fish, scallops and shrimp are kept on ice ready for you to buy. To go along with that, pick up some bottled sauces, beer or a nice bottle of wine, and a few of the groceries you'll need. In true island fashion, JoBob's doubles as a souvenir store and also offers bait and tackle and beach accessories.

Shoreline Beach Mart

24202 Hwy. 12, Rodanthe
                      (252) 987-1403

Whatever you need for your beach, camping or fishing trip, you can get it here. They've got groceries, bait, tackle, gifts and souvenirs, supplies, firewood, ice, drinks and more.

Village Video

Pamlico Station, Hwy. 12,
Rodanthe   (252) 987-2988

For those rainy days and mellow nights at home, Village Video rents movies of every genre for every age group. Village Video has the best selection of new releases on Hatteras Island. VHS and DVD movie rentals are available. Vacationers are welcome, and no membership is required. They also rent PlayStation II.

Hatteras T-Shirt Outlet and Island Gift Shop

Pamlico Station, Hwy. 12,
  Rodanthe   (252) 987-1404

You'll find a little bit of everything at this store. There are tons of T-shirts, imprinted with Outer Banks and Hatteras Island themes or with your own custom lettering, and they have a special deal where you can get three Ts for $9.99. Hermit crabs, gifts and souvenirs are also available.

Exotic Cargo Home Outfitters

Pamlico Station, Hwy. 12,
Rodanthe   (252) 987-2141

For the exotic and unusual, don't miss Exotic Cargo. This store features furniture (including teak furniture), a multitude of home accessories, clothing, jewelry, toys, wooden boxes, animal and exotic sculpture and more, all imported from the far corners of the world.

Surfside Casuals and Suits Galore

Pamlico Station, Hwy. 12,
Rodanthe   (252) 987-1414

With seven stores along the Outer Banks, Surfside Casuals is one of the area's most well-known names in beach apparel and sportswear. Surfside Casuals offers some of the hottest brand names

See **www.hatterasguide.com** for full content, links & updates.

A New Shopping Complex Serving Rodanthe, Waves and Salvo at the Gateway to Hatteras Island!

Adjacent to the Post Office in Rodanthe, St. Waves Plaza is home to fine retailers such as Kitty Hawk Kites, Ocean Annie's, Just for the Beach, Seafood & Stuff and Island Pizza & Steam Bar.

FOR MORE INFORMATION CALL:
252-207-3400
RAVA
PO Box 3009
Kitty Hawk, NC 27949

in surf- and beach-inspired clothing for women, men and children. The swimsuit section, Suits Galore, lives up to its name with hundreds of suits, including separates, for every shape and age.

Ocean Gourmet and Gifts

23753 Hwy. 12,
Rodanthe   (252) 987-1166

When you've got some spare time to browse around the shops of Rodanthe, don't miss a visit to Ocean Gourmet and Gifts. There are lots of fun souvenirs here, including lighthouse collectibles, figurines, jewelry, mugs, key chains and more. You'll find some beach-inspired clothes and swimsuits. Try some candy, ice cream or fudge before you leave.

Reef

Hwy. 12, Rodanthe   (252) 987-2821

Reef offers stuff you'll need for the beach, plus lots of souvenirs. You'll find towels, chairs, hats, rafts, sunglasses & toys. You can also get henna tattoos and novelty T-shirts.

Dare Building Supply

Hwy. 12, Waves   (252) 987-2744

This big store isn't just for contractors and builders. They also offer beach goods, housewares, RV and camping supplies, toys, flags and other items a vacationer might need.

Michael Halminski Photo Gallery

Hwy. 12, Waves   (252) 987-2401

Michael Halminski is one of the Outer Banks' most talented photographers. His photographs of birds, wildlife, water, sky and local scenes perfectly capture the mood of Hatteras Island. Photographs and note cards are available for sale at his island studio. Call before stopping by.

Kitty Hawk Kites

St. Waves Plaza, Hwy. 12, Waves
(252) 987-1100   (877) FLY-THIS

Kitty Hawk Kites specializes in kites, from the kiddie kind to high-tech stunt varieties. The store also sells fun things like flags, toys, boomerangs and games. You'll also find casual apparel, T-shirts, hats and sunglasses for outdoor-minded men and women.

Ocean Annie's

St. Waves Plaza, N.C. Hwy. 12,
Waves   (252) 987-2109

Ocean Annie's, a longtime fixture on

See www.hatterasguide.com for full content, links & updates.

the Outer Banks shopping scene, opened its newest gallery here in 2004. Functional and decorative pottery is the specialty, especially the work of Bill Campbell. You'll also find jewelry, wind chimes, candles, stained glass, neat wooden boxes, the popular Peggy Karr fused glass plates, gourmet coffee beans and much more.

Just For The Beach
St. Waves Plaza, Hwy. 12,
Waves   (252) 987-9939
You don't have to bring everything with you on vacation. Rent it when you get here. Just For The Beach rents recreational equipment like bikes, kayaks, surfboards and baby joggers; entertainment equipment like DVD players, TVs and stereos; beach gear like umbrellas, chairs and carts; baby furniture like cribs and high chairs; and appliances like gas grills and roll-away beds.

Seafood 'N Stuff
St. Waves Plaza, Hwy. 12,
Waves   (252) 987-1222
If you're looking for good eats in the Tri-Village area, look no further. Seafood & Stuff is a seafood market selling fresh fish, shrimp, crab, crab legs, clams, oysters and more, and you can get your shrimp and crab legs steamed to go. You can also take home Clam Bake steamer pots complete with seafood, vegetables and condiments. All you have to do is pick it up, take it home and steam it on your stove. Seafood & Stuff also sells deli meats, cheeses, desserts, fresh fruits and vegetables, beer and wine. Everything is available for take-out only.

See **www.hatterasguide.com** for full content, links & updates.

pottery
jewelry
wood
metalwork
glass
chimes
gourmet
coffee
beans

Ocean Annie's
Featuring contemporary crafts from dozens of U.S. artisans

Island Shoppes
AVON
995.4644

St. Waves Plaza
WAVES
987.2109

Mattress Mart II Sleep Emporium

Tarang Corner, Hwy. 12,
Waves　　　　　　　(252) 987-9937

Mattress Mart makes it easy to outfit rental homes and cottages on Hatteras Island. They offer mattresses by Sealy Posturpedic, Tempurpedic and Simmons BeautyRest plus bed frames, headboards, footboards, bunk beds, futons and other bedroom furniture. They offer free delivery on Hatteras and Ocracoke islands.

The Blue Whale

Hwy. 12, Salvo　　　　　(252) 987-2335

The Blue Whale has been in business on Hatteras Island for more than 30 years. They sell gas, groceries, beer and wine, novelties, hot sauces and T-shirts, bait and tackle, beach supplies, books and magazines and more.

The Fishin' Hole

Sand St., Salvo　　　　　(252) 987-2351

In business since the 1970s, The Fishin' Hole is a full-service tackle shop with live bait (including live eels) and tackle plus brand-name rods and reels. It is an official weigh station, and the staff repairs rods and reels. They also sell groceries, snacks and drinks, beach supplies, T-shirts, waders, hip boots and clothing.

Salvo Market Marina and Campground

Hwy. 12, Salvo　　　　　(252) 987-2288

The gas station at the south end of Salvo has a lot going on. Inside you'll find snacks, drinks and a few necessity items plus food for breakfast and lunch, including homemade biscuits. Out back is a small campground plus a boat launch and dock.

Avon

Ocean Annie's Craft Gallery

Island Shops, Hwy. 12,
Avon　　　　　　　　(252) 995-4644

Ocean Annie's has been a longtime fixture on the Outer Banks shopping scene, and it's a gallery that people return to year after year. Functional and decorative pottery is the specialty, especially the work of Bill Campbell. You'll also find jewelry, wind chimes, candles, stained glass, neat wooden boxes, the popular Peggy Karr fused glass plates and gourmet coffee beans.

Kitty Hawk Kites/ Carolina Outdoors

Island Shops, Hwy. 12, Avon
(252) 995-6060　　　　(877) FLY-THIS

As the name suggests, Kitty Hawk Kites specializes in kites, from the kiddie kind to

high-tech stunt varieties. The store also sells flags, toys, boomerangs and games. Carolina Outdoors is the outfitter side of the store, selling casual apparel, T-shirts, hats and sunglasses for outdoor-minded men and women.

Fisherman's Daughter
Hwy. 12, Avon   (252) 995-6148

Be prepared for some serious shopping. Fisherman's Daughter offers a great assortment of goods, from OBX and HI gear to Vera Bradley bags and Yankee Candles. Downstairs you'll find jewelry, swimwear, hats and clothing, including Mudd and Tommy Hilfiger jeans, Flax women's wear and swimsuits. Upstairs is a gallery with artwork, books, collectibles, lighthouse figurines, Christmas items and much more.

Nags Head Hammocks
Hwy. 12, Avon   (252) 995-3744

Nags Head Hammocks have been handcrafted on the Outer Banks since 1974. The rope hammocks, hammock swings and chairs are a favorite souvenir that will put you in a vacation mood all year long. The ropes, wood and hardware used in Nags Head Hammocks are weather-resistant, so these hammocks hold up extremely well and last a very long time. Stop by the store to see the hammocks being crafted onsite.

The Glass Bead
Dairy Queen Shopping Center, Hwy. 12, Avon   (252) 995-7020

Let your creative streak shine at this make-your-own jewelry store. The Glass Bead has hundreds of beads, including handmade ones, crystals, semiprecious stones, charms and seed beads, plus hemp

See **www.hatterasguide.com** for full content, links & updates.

for designing your own necklaces, bracelets, earrings and other jewelry. You can make the jewelry here, and lessons are offered. All the supplies you need are available, including books. Check out the new coffee shop and Internet café next door.

Zofia's Art Gallery
Dairy Queen Shopping Center,
Hwy. 12, Avon   (252) 995-7871

Zofia Lategano is a lively artist, and her fun gallery reflects her personality. Her specialties are painting — oils, acrylics, watercolors — and photography. She also does fish prints (using real fish her husband catches). You'll find her work alongside the artworks of other locals, including a print maker, map maker, painters, potters and jewelry designers. Zofia offers art classes to kids, including painting and fish printing.

Sailworld
Dairy Queen Shopping Center,
Hwy. 12, Avon   (252) 995-5441

Sailworld is a full-service windsurfing and kite-boarding shop, and they sell new and used gear for both sports. They offer a full range of boards, sails, rig components, accessories, wetsuits, fins, hardware and spare parts. You can try many models before you buy. The store also sells backpacks, streetwear, swimwear, sunglasses and pretty much anything else the active crowd needs.

Frank and Fran's
Hwy. 12, Avon   (252) 995-4171

This tackle shop calls itself the "Fisherman's Friend" because it offers everything an angler could need, including fine cigars for those times when the bite is slow. Frank and Fran's sells bait and tackle, fishing supplies and gear, ice and much more. Stop by for fishing advice

See www.hatterasguide.com for full content, links & updates.

and for information on Cape Hatteras Anglers Club tournaments. This is an official weigh station.

Dockside Hatteras
Hwy. 12, Avon   (252) 995-5445

Dockside Hatteras specializes in beach-home decor. They sell furniture, including sofas, chairs, tables, barstools, beds and chests, plus home necessities like mattresses, colorful shower curtains, bath mats, pots and pans, dishes, glasses, dish towels and more. Home accents are available too, such as end tables, mirrors, framed prints, lamps, rugs and throw pillows. It's a great place to find gifts. Dockside Hatteras delivers for free.

Island Spice and Wine
Hwy. 12, Avon   (252) 995-7750

Your taste buds will love you for visiting this store. The wine selection is vast and pleasantly surprising, with numerous worthy selections from California and around the world. You'll also find fine tea and coffee, specialty sauces, hard-to-find spices, imported olive oils and vinegars, cheese, crackers, bread, sweets, chocolates, mixes, gourmet snacks and many other things that will inspire a night of gourmet cooking. The store also sells cookbooks, dishes, glasses, aprons, utensils and other kitchen-related items. Gifts and gift baskets are available.

Breeze Thru Avon
40374 Hwy. 12, Avon (252) 995-3347

This drive-through beverage store offers drinks and beer of all varieties, and you never have to leave your car to get it. The staff person brings it to you. They sell gas and ice too.

Mill Creek Gifts
40374Hwy. 12, Avon   (252) 995-3188

This gift shop, in the same building as the Breeze Thru, sells ornaments, home accents, local artwork, seashells, stained glass, wind chimes and other items that add a sparkle to any home's decor. They also sell jewelry and saltwater taffy.

Home Port Gifts
Hwy. 12, Avon   (252) 995-4334

The aromatic smell of potpourri greets you at Home Port Gifts. You can buy several scents of potpourri plus candles, baskets, artwork, seashells, chimes, nautical gifts and antiques, stained glass, lighthouses, cards and much more. You'll love the selection of silver jewelry here. If you're looking for a gift, this is the place to find one. This store is in the same building as Cape Hatteras Realty.

"Food Is Good!" VILLAGE GROCERY

A *new island tradition*!

- Certified Angus Beef
- Finest Local Seafood
- Boar's Head Deli Meats
- Gourmet Salads
- Delicious Sandwiches
- Fresh Produce
- Gourmet Salad Bar
- Fresh Breads & Desserts
- Wines & Cheeses

**Village Grocery:
252-995-4402
Kinnakeet Corner:
252-995-7011**
*Both located at the first traffic light on
Highway 12 South, in Avon Village*

"Supplies for Island Life"

KINNAKEET CORNER

Most everything you need!

- Convenience store
- Quality Pure gasoline
- Beach toys & boogie boards
- Beach chairs & towels
- Tackle & bait
- Island wear
- Souvenirs

HOT STUFF FOOD ON THE GO

*Delicious,
fast food!*

- *Angus Beef Burgers*
- *Breakfast Biscuits & Burritos*
- *Grilled or Crispy Chicken*
- *Pizza and More!*

Studio 12 Paint Our Pottery

Hwy. 12, Avon   (252) 995-7899

When you're looking for something to do beyond the beach, get creative at this pottery-painting studio. You select an item, paint it to your heart's content, and they'll fire and glaze it for you to pick up later in the week. It's open Monday through Saturday.

The Village Grocery

Hwy. 12, Avon   (252) 995-4402

The Village Grocery is the purveyor of all the fine food items you'll need to stock your vacation-home kitchen. It sells fresh seafood and produce plus fine wines and cheeses. A butcher is on staff, specializing in Angus beef. There's also a deli featuring Boar's Head meats. This is a full-service grocery store, and the salad bar is an extra reason to come here.

Kinnakeet Corner

Hwy. 12 and Harbor Dr., Avon
          (252) 995-7011

This corner convenience store says it offers "supplies for the island life." They sell gasoline, groceries, snacks, drinks, beer and wine, beach supplies, bait and tackle, souvenirs and gifts. There's also an ATM here. It's at the northern stoplight in Avon.

Stoney's Seafood

40658 Hwy. 12, Avon (252) 995-6132

Stop by Stoney's for fresh, local seafood, including fish, clams, scallops, oysters, crabs and shrimp. You'll also find Texaco gasoline, bait and tackle, gifts, drinks, and beach supplies.

See **www.hatterasguide.com** for full content, links & updates.

Gaskins Gallery

40462 North End Rd., Avon
(252) 995-6617

It's worth the trip back into the older area of Avon to find this gallery. Turn west on Harbor Road (at the stoplight) then take a right on North End Road. The gallery is in a new, cedar-shake house a little ways down on the left. The first and second floor gallery rooms are open and spacious, with room to stand back and admire the artwork. You'll find paintings and pottery by local artists, prints, photography, Fenton art glass, jewelry and other works of art. Gaskins Gallery specializes in framing.

Country Elegance

Harbor Rd., Avon   (252) 995-6269

Country Elegance is in a little cottage in the quiet part of Avon, and the shop is so warm and homey it makes you want to linger. In business for 15 years, the shop specializes in dainty and beautiful lace. You'll find lace curtains and valances, lace clothing, embroidered lace wall hangings and more. Also look for hats, clothing, baskets, candles, cross-stitch crafts, ornaments and other items that will lend an elegant country flair to your home.

Deep Blue

Hwy. 12, Avon   (252) 986-1211

This mega-store sells everything you need for the beach — towels, swim suits, body boards, rafts and toys. You'll also find lots of souvenirs and novelty items. It's next to Stoney's Seafood, as if you could miss it.

Ocean Atlantic Rentals

Hwy. 12, Avon
(252) 995-5868   (800) 635-9559

Ocean Atlantic Rentals specializes in items that vacationers don't want to bring with them. Strollers, baby equipment, wheelchairs, roll-away beds, umbrellas, beach chairs, beach cabanas, bicycles for the whole family, volleyball nets, DVD players and VCRs, movie rentals and much more. They even deliver. Advance reservations are recommended.

T-Shirt Whirl

Hwy. 12, Avon   (252) 995-4111

Located next to Ocean Atlantic Rentals, T-Shirt Whirl has you covered in the T-shirt department. Choose from one of a jillion designs, or design your own with decals and letters.

Sweet & Sassy

Hwy. 12, Avon   (252) 995-5647

In the orange building next to The Pickled Palm, Sweet & Sassy is a women's boutique full of items for pampering yourself or someone you love. You'll find lovely lingerie and pajamas, sundresses and other summer wear, jewelry, luscious body products, including Burt's Bees, hand-painted glassware and other gift items.

Village Video

Hwy. 12, Avon   (252) 995-5138

Village Video rents DVDs and VHS movies at four locations on Hatteras Island. They offer a great selection of new releases plus the classics that you want to watch again and again. Vacationers are welcome, and no membership is required. They also rent PlayStation II.

Mad Mad Hatteras

Hwy. 12, Avon   (252) 995-6873

Mad Mad Hatteras is a one-stop shopping extravaganza featuring art-to-wear, clothing, fabulous footwear and all sorts of accessories for your beach house and home. There are gifts aplenty from artful to zany, bubbly bath and body, and a fountain of other fun stuff. Funky barware, Silvestri decorative pieces, Sandra Magsamen artwork, fantastic fashions and gifts for every occasion are highlights. Look for the store in the heart of Avon next to Nino's Pizza.

Surf's Up Seafood Market

Hwy. 12, Avon   (252) 995-3432

Feel like cooking in tonight? Surf's Up sells fresh fish, shrimp, clams, scallops and other seafood. Surf's Up will steam shrimp and seafood for you if you'd like.

Ocean Threads Beachwear

Hatteras Island Plaza,
Hwy. 12, Avon   (252) 995-9099

With several locations on the Outer Banks, Ocean Threads is a favorite for surf-inspired streetwear for men and women. They carry swimwear for both men and women as well, plus sunglasses, body jewelry and an awesome selection of sandals and flip flops. Shop here for skateboards and equipment.

Surfside Casuals and Suits Galore

Hatteras Island Plaza,
Hwy. 12, Avon   (252) 995-5577

Everybody can find a swimsuit at this store. The variety of styles and sizes is amazing, and separates are available for those who have trouble finding a suit that fits. You'll also find clothing for men, women and children plus sandals, T-shirts, sweatshirts and more.

Food Lion

Hatteras Island Plaza,
Hwy. 12, Avon   (252) 995-4488

Food Lion is a major chain grocery store, the largest on the island. They offer fresh produce, a bakery, hot foods and all the grocery items you'll need, but you'll have to get your fresh seafood somewhere else.

Try My Nuts Nut Company

Hatteras Island Plaza,
Hwy. 12, Avon   (252) 995-7000

Feeling a little nutty? This store sells delicious nuts, including gourmet roasted nuts, chocolate-covered nuts, honey-roasted nuts and others in all flavors and varieties. They also sell chocolates, candy, popcorn, cookie mixes, drink mixes, T-shirts and an incredible assortment of hot sauces.

Ace Hardware
Hatteras Island Plaza,
Hwy. 12, Avon   (252) 995-6600
    Ace Hardware sells everything for the home, garden and yard. Most people know it's the place to find tools, paint and hardware, but you may not know they sell deck furniture, cleaning supplies, kitchen supplies, bathroom accessories, beach supplies, baskets, frames, pet supplies and much more.

Exotic Cargo
Hatteras Island Plaza,
Hwy. 12, Avon   (252) 995-7702
    For unique gifts and home decor, everyone loves browsing at Exotic Cargo. All the goods in this store are imported from the far corners of the world. You'll find clothing, jewelry, bags, rugs, furniture, exotic masks and animal sculpture, frames, wooden toys and more.

Beach Pharmacy
Hatteras Island Plaza,
Hwy. 12, Avon   (252) 995-3811
    This Good Neighbor Pharmacy fill prescriptions, plus it offers a variety of over-the-counter medicines, sundries, beach supplies, office supplies and more.

Sew Many Things
Hatteras Island Plaza,
Hwy. 12, Avon   (252) 995-4007
    Sew Many Things is a gift shop offering a variety of items. You'll find shells, souvenirs, lighthouses, jewelry, stained glass and glass items plus clothes.

Sea Treasures
Hatteras Island Plaza,
Hwy. 12, Avon   (252) 995-7800
    Sea Treasures offers beach-themed gifts for everyone, whether you want inexpensive souvenirs or high-end treasures. This store sells swimwear, clothes, T-shirts and sweatshirts, and tons of souvenirs.

Askins Creek Store
Hwy. 12, Avon   (252) 995-6283
    The southernmost commercial business in Avon, just north of Canadian Hole, this store sells necessities and fun stuff. Gas (BP-Amoco and diesel), beer and wine, groceries, snacks, beach items, sunscreen, bait and tackle, ice, beach toys, T-shirts, local interest books, maps, charts, cards, souvenirs, gifts and flags are just some of the things you'll find here.

See **www.hatterasguide.com** for full content, links & updates.

Askins Creek also has an automatic car wash with undercarriage and a manual car wash. Money orders and money wiring services are available.

Buxton

Day Dreams Clothing
Hwy. 12, Buxton   (252) 995-5548

The stylish girl's dream come true. Sister store to a Charlottesville, Virginia, Day Dreams, this store combines the best of city chic with the best of island style. You'll find swimwear for everyone, sundresses, flip flops and sunglasses, as well as designer dresses and separates, jewelry, nice accessories and a great selection of fall and winter clothes. We love the selection of hats and purses. The sale rack alone is worth devoting some serious time to.

Surfside Casuals
Hwy. 12, Buxton   (252) 995-3352

This store, part of a local chain of swim- and sportswear stores, specializes in make-your-own T-shirts and sweatshirts.

Dillon's Corner
Hwy. 12, Buxton   (252) 995-5083

This is really two stores in one. Downstairs it's a tackle shop, with bait, tackle, rods and reels, gas, gear, waders, boots, snacks, rod and reel repair, custom-rod building, rental tackle, tide charts and everything else for fishermen. Upstairs it's a gift shop and gallery, with artwork, prints, ceramics, Yankee Candles, local interest books, novelties, wind chimes, lighthouse figurines, T-shirts and many other gifts and souvenirs.

The Red Drum

Hwy. 12, Buxton   (252) 995-5414

The legendary Red Drum, serving Hatteras Island since 1954, does just about everything. All housed in a long strip on the east side of Highway 12 are a tackle shop, a beach supply and grocery store, a gas station, an auto parts store and an auto repair shop. The tackle shop offers all the bait, tackle, supplies, gear and advice you'll need, plus rod building and repair. Then you can run over to get all the groceries you'll need for the trip. Texaco gas is sold here.

Risky Business Seafood Market

Hwy. 12, Buxton   (252) 995-4211

Look here for the freshest seafood, including shrimp, clams, crab, fish, scallops and more. Risky Business handles its seafood with care so you'll know it's fresh and safe to eat.

The Cottage Shop

Hwy. 12, Buxton   (252) 995-3960

You can't miss this place – in a shockingly yellow building near the lighthouse entrance – and you wouldn't want to. This is one of three locations of The Cottage Shop, which has become an Outer Banks favorite for seaside home decor and wedding gifts. From the functional to the decorative, there are items for the kitchen, bath, dining room, bedroom, porch and garden. If you need to outfit an entire rental cottage, The Cottage Shop specializes in packages.

Light Keeper Gallery

Hwy. 12, Buxton   (252) 995-4435

Artists Stephanie Kiker Geib and Scott Geib perfectly capture the mood

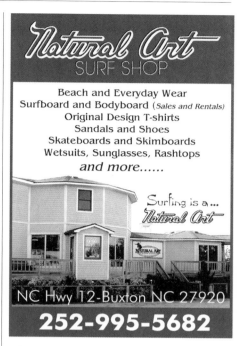
of Hatteras Island and Buxton in their artwork, and this gallery is the place to take it all in. Scott's photographs of local scenes are stunning, including the famous shot of the moon rising behind the lighthouse. Stephanie's vivid painted images are available as prints or on tiles, magnets, clocks, trivets, T-shirts, switchplates and more.

Village Video

Buxton Back Rd., Buxton
                    (252) 995-6227

For the latest and greatest in movies, visit Village Video. Village Video rents DVDs and VHS movies at four locations on Hatteras Island. They offer a great selection of new releases plus the classics that you want to watch again and again. Vacationers are welcome, and no membership is required. They also rent PlayStation II.

Sweet Street
Hwy. 12, Buxton   (252) 995-6649

In the heart of Buxton right down the street from the lighthouse, Sweet Street offers a chance to indulge your sweet tooth and your love of island history. This candy shop is located in a historic home that was moved, floated over the sound from Avon to Buxton actually, after a great storm in 1833. Look for the house tucked beneath beautiful old trees. Sweet Street sells candy only – fudge, saltwater taffy, old-fashioned favorites, and lots of chocolate, including seashore shapes like shells and fish. You'll ooh and aah over the treats in this colorful store, which is truly a delight to the senses. It's open seasonally so call before you go in the off-season.

Hotline Thrift Shops
Hwy. 12, Buxton   (252) 986-1332

Whether you're donating used items or looking for something new-to-you, supporting this shop helps raise funds for Hotline, a crisis line, shelter and domestic violence prevention service for women and children. The thrift shop accepts and sells clothes, books, magazines, home accessories and appliances, furniture, baby items, toys and much morewill keep you here browsing for quite some time, and you'll want to stay awhile and talk with the friendly owners.

Woods Oceanic Art
Hwy. 12, Buxton   (252) 995-6165

This art gallery specializes in local artwork. Buxton artist Kim Mosher sells her very popular prints and tiles here. You'll also find surf art and other creations from the local talent pool.

Natural Art Surf Shop
Hwy. 12, Buxton   (252) 995-5682

Natural Art has been a fixture on the island surfing scene since 1977, and it's all about serious surfing. They shape custom boards and create custom artwork . They sell new and used boards and rent surf boards, body boards and wetsuits. They also repair surfboards. All the surfing support gear is here too: clothing, footwear, wetsuits, rash guards, accessories, sunscreen, art, you name it. If you need inspiration, check out their surf video rentals.

Ocean Notions
Osprey Shopping Center,
Hwy. 12, Buxton   (252) 995-4335

Ocean Notions is a fun place to spend some time. They offer gifts and souvenirs, jewelry, clothes, swimsuits, board shorts, T-shirts, sandals and other things you need for the vacation lifestyle.

See **www.hatterasguide.com** for full content, links & updates.

A small store, packed with good books

Contemporary Fiction | **Southern Fiction**
Kids and Young Adults | **Outer Banks**
Cook Books | **and Field Guides**
Murder Mysteries | **Women's Interests**
Health and Awareness | **Sea Stories**

Buxton Village Books
Open All Year
252-995-4240 • bvb2@mindspring.com
Mail orders welcome

Conner's Supermarket
Hwy. 12, Buxton   (252) 995-5711

Family owned and operated on Hatteras Island for more than 45 years, Conner's is a full-service grocery store that caters to locals and visitors. They offer a wide selection of items, from everyday necessities to gourmet treats. There's a large selection of meats and produce, and the deli counter offers meats, cheeses and hot-food specials to take away. Beach items and souvenirs are also available here.

The Old Gray House
Light Plant Rd.,
Buxton   (252) 995-6098

The Old Gray House is one of those stores that vacationers can't wait to return to each year. It is housed in an historic island home (see site 31 on the Historic Tour). Inside you'll find tons of treasures

and gifts, much of it handcrafted. Christmas decorations, baskets, wreaths, cross-stitch, woodwork, birdhouses, dolls, knickknacks, potpourri, plants, garden statuary, birdbaths, shells, lots of lighthouses and more. It's between the post office and the school.

Island Dollar
Hwy. 12, Buxton   (252) 995-7755

Hatteras Island's own version of the dollar store sells all kinds of stuff - toys, cards, balloons, gift bags, holiday decorations, home supplies and so much more. And everything really is $1.

Buxton Village Books
Hwy. 12, Buxton   (252) 995-4240

At this bookstore you get to wander around in a charming old cottage with sloping, creaky floors. The owner, Gee Gee Rosell, has a welcoming smile and great taste in books. Look for cookbooks, local-interest books and music, fiction, nonfiction, best-sellers, a great selection of Southern fiction, mysteries, field guides, half-price used books, unique greeting cards and note cards, journals and much more. It's open year round.

Caper's Light
Hwy. 12, Buxton   (252) 995-6011

This gift shop offers a great variety. You'll find stained glass, flags, hammocks, jewelry, nautical items, hats, T-shirts and lots of lighthouses. It's between the post office and the school.

Hatteras Island Toy Store
Geo Gaskins Lane,
Buxton   (252) 995-7171

Now in a new location just past the Fish House Restaurant, the Hatteras

Island Toy Store offers the best selection of educational and fun toys on the island. You'll find the currently popular toys like Thomas the Tank Engine, Beanie Babies and Groovy Girls, plus imaginative toys like music and musical instruments, art supplies, dress-up clothes, puppets, games, puzzles and more. There's also a good selection of baby toys.

Buxton Seafood

Hwy. 12, Buxton   (252) 995-5085

Buxton Seafood offers the freshest food straight from the sea. Fish, clams, shrimp, scallops, oysters, crabs and more are available from this shop, where you can always trust the quality. They also sell grocery items, including steaks and sauces, plus gift items. You'll find it next to the water tower.

See **www.hatterasguide.com** for full content, links & updates.

Frisco

Islander Gifts

Hwy. 12, Frisco   (252) 995-5427

When you're zipping down Highway 12 into Frisco, don't miss this shop, the first one in the village. The shop carries an amazing selection of gifts and souvenirs, from glass and wood carvings to jewelry, T-shirts and driftwood. The selection of seashells and specimen shells is impressive, and there are nautical-inspired home-decor items, pirate toys, Christmas ornaments, bird carvings and more.

Indian Town Gallery and Gifts

Hwy. 12, Frisco   (252) 995-5181

Indian Town Gallery has moved to a new location next to Island Perks Coffee Shop (just south of the old location), but it still has the same great premise — all of the art and craft is made by Outer Banks artists, the majority of them from the island. One look in here and you'll be convinced that the gift of creativity is abundant by the sea. This is the place to look for highly original works of art – paintings, ceramics, jewelry, woodworks, photographs, blown glass, baskets, handmade journals and more. Most days you'll find native painter Wayne Fulcher at work here.

Scotch Bonnet Candies and Gifts

Hwy. 12, Frisco   (252) 995-4242

Need something sweet? Scotch Bonnet offers a great selection of candies, ice cream and fudge to satisfy any sweet tooth. On any given day you can find 25 varieties of homemade fudge plus four or five sugar-free flavors. They also offer jams and jellies, shells, hermit crabs, beach supplies, fireworks, T-shirts and a variety of other gifts.

Island Windblocks / Hawaiian Party Shop

Hwy. 12, Frisco   (252) 995-9990

Why let wind ruin an otherwise great day, whether you're relaxing at the beach, grilling, camping or just need privacy? An Island Windblock is the perfect solution. Rentals are $9 a day or $35 a week. Several sizes are available for purchase starting at $29.95. While you're here, check out the Hawaiian Party Shop. Here you'll find everything for an island-style luau – from coconut bras, leis and hula skirts for her to Hawaiian shirts at great prices for him. Decorations, tiki torches, string lights, lighted palm trees, flamingos, tropical wall art, parrots, geckos, fish, frogs . . . it's all here.

See **www.hatterasguide.com** for full content, links & updates.

Red Drum Pottery

Hwy. 12, Frisco   (252) 995-5757

This is the working studio of potters Wes Lassiter and Rhonda Bates. You can often catch the potters at the wheel, and you can see their functional and decorative pieces on display in the gallery. There's a painting gallery here as well, representing Rhonda and several other local painters. From June through September, they open their theater for the very special Frisco Jubilee, an opry-style show featuring local musicians, poets and personalities (see the Recreation chapter).

Sea Weeds Garden Shop

Hwy. 12, Frisco   (252) 995-5702

Sea Weeds is a cool little shop in an older cottage. The front yard is filled with plants for sale, and the cottage is stocked with antiques and fun things, including artwork, rugs, pottery and garden accessories.

Frisco Tackle

Hwy. 12, Frisco   (252) 995-4361

Frisco Tackle offers everything you need for fishing — bait and tackle, gear, ice, drinks, rod and reel rentals, clam rake rentals and more. You'll also find a good selection of gifts and T-shirts.

This Little Cottage

Hwy. 12, Frisco   (252) 995-3320

If you're into home furnishings and decor, this store is for you. They carry lots of brand names in home furnishings, all with coastal cottage flair. Some you'll recognize are Maine Cottage and Shabby Chic furnishings, Lexington, Pine Cone Hill bedding, Vietri and Fioriware pottery.

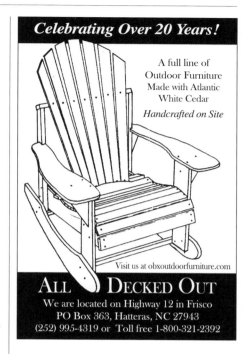
But there's more than furniture, fabric and home décor. You'll find candles, home-care products and great gifts. They also specialize in kitchen and bath cabinetry.

Frisco Woods Campstore

Hwy. 12, Frisco   (252) 995-5208

This is the ultimate campground store, but it's much more than that. They sell all the necessities, such as ice, drinks, snacks, gas, film, groceries, beach and camping supplies, hot coffee, beer and wine, and ice cream, but they also feature local books, puzzles, games, gifts, T-shirts and souvenirs. Stop in to ask about windsurfing and kayaking lessons and rentals and to inquire about the campground.

Browning's

Hwy. 12, Frisco   (252) 995-5538

Browning's is a well-respected art gallery representing high-caliber American artists and craftspeople, with a selection that's rich with distinctive works. Unusual handcrafted jewelry for men and women is Browning's specialty, and there's also an impressive selection of art glass. Works in metal, wood and photography are also offered. Gift registry and shipping services are available.

All Decked Out

Hwy. 12, Frisco
(252) 995-4319   (800) 321-2392

All Decked Out has a full line of handmade outdoor furniture, including Adirondack chairs and rockers, loungers, picnic tables, swings and more. All furniture is made of Atlantic white cedar. Delivery is available from Corolla to

Ocracoke, and they ship if you can't get it home.

Frisco Rod & Gun

Hwy. 12, Frisco   (252) 995-5366

Frisco Rod & Gun offers all the goods for the avid outdoor sportsman. Guns, hunting gear, clothing, fishing rods, fly fishing and conventional tackle, bait, waders, sunglasses, binoculars – you name it, it's here. It's also a convenience store selling Texaco gas, snacks, drinks and a good selection of groceries and beach toys.

Hatteras Village

Family Jewels

Hwy. 12,
Hatteras Village   (252) 986-2323

What a perfect setup: Not only can you watch Family Jewels' owner Wendy Sisler making her glasswork beads, but you can also buy her beautiful, handcrafted jewelry that incorporates glass beads, pearls, gem stones, crystals and other stunning baubles. Sisler also sells an incredible assortment of silver charms and pendants.

Sandy Bay Gallery

Hwy. 12,
Hatteras Village   (252) 986-1338

Sandy Bay Gallery is a place of pure creativity, with unique, original fine artwork by locals and artists from around the country. You'll find jewelry, paintings, blown glass, sculpture, ceramics and much more. Popular Buxton artist Kim Mosher's tiles and prints are sold here, along with originals by a variety of artists.

Izabelle's Closet

Hwy. 12,
Hatteras Village　　　　(252) 986-6575

This is one of the best clothing stores on the island. Whether you're looking for something flirty and casual to wear on the island or something a little more upscale to wear back home, you'll find it here. Izabelle's Closet has a good selection of Flax clothing and other flowy pants, dresses and skirts. They also sell great accessories — jewelry, bags, shoes, sunglasses — plus some T-shirts and workout wear. April Cornell children's clothes are also popular here. It shares space with Sandy Bay Gallery, making this a fun one-stop shop.

Beach Pharmacy of Hatteras

Hwy. 12,
Hatteras Village　　　　(252) 986-2400

Beach Pharmacy provides a full-service pharmacy plus all the over-counter medications, necessities and sundries you'll need. It's on the north end of Buxton, next to Village Video.

Village Video

Hwy. 12,
Hatteras Village　　　　(252) 986-2181

Village Video has the best selection of new releases on Hatteras Island. VHS and DVD movie rentals are available. Vacationers are welcome, and no membership is required. They also rent PlayStation II.

Creative Ballance

Hwy. 12,
Hatteras Village　　　　(252) 986-2154

Creative Ballance is a full-service salon offering a full range of hair services and products. They also do nails: manicures, pedicures, gel and acrylic nails, and hand-painted nail art. If you're looking for

See **www.hatterasguide.com** for full content, links & updates.

tanning beds, this is the place to come.

Angler's Headquarters
Hwy. 12,
Hatteras Village   (252) 986-2989
Angler's HQ is in the old Austin store in the heart of the village. You can't miss it, in the white historic home by the supermarket and the fire station. They sell tackle, bait and gear and build custom rods, reels and rigs. You can also find ice, snacks and various other items here.

Burrus Red & White Supermarket
Hwy. 12, Hatteras Village (252) 986-2333
Burrus has been serving Hatteras Villagers for more than a century — since 1866! It's a full-service grocery store with fresh meats, seafood and produce, necessities and specialty products. The people are always friendly here, and it's open year round.

The Old Station – A Convenient Stop
Hwy. 12, Hatteras Village (252) 986-2468
The Old Station sells all the necessities: Texaco gas, snacks, candy, drinks, beer, wine, ice, ice cream, coffee, pizza, doughnuts and beach supplies.

Nedo Shopping Center
Hwy. 12, Hatteras Village (252) 986-2545
The Nedo store is like an old-fashioned variety store inside a modern building. Like the sign says, you'll find a little bit of everything. The shelves are lined with hardware and do-it-yourself supplies, yard tools, cleaning products, house wares and home decor, fishing supplies, toys, souvenirs, craft supplies, clothes, cards and lots more.

Outer Banks Diving
Hwy. 12,
Hatteras Village   (252) 986-1056
Outer Banks Diving (see the Recreation chapter for information about scuba diving charters) sells snorkeling gear, scuba gear, wetsuits, accessories, T-shirts and apparel of interest to divers. But even if you don't dive you should stop by this store to see their variety of unique souvenirs. Outer Banks Diving sells giant prehistoric shark's teeth plus shipwreck and nautical items, some for souvenir hunters, others for serious collectors.

Risky Business Seafood Market
Oden's Dock, Hwy. 12,
Hatteras Village   (252) 986-2117
For the freshest shrimp, fish, scallops, crabs and clams, Risky Business is a trusted name in seafood. They'll steam up spiced shrimp or crabs for you to take out if you don't want to cook yourself. Risky Business also offers complete processing of your catch, from cleaning to vacuum packaging to freezing.

Summer Stuff
Hwy. 12,
Hatteras Village   (252) 986-2280
Stop at Summer Stuff to pick up all the things you'll want on vacation. You'll find clothing, swimsuits and T-shirts, gifts and souvenirs, jewelry, sunglasses, beach gear, toys, towels, seashells, fireworks and more. It's right next to Midgett Realty in the heart of the village.

See **www.hatterasguide.com** for full content, links & updates.

A **Hatteras Village** Tradition since 1948

LEE ROBINSON GENERAL STORE — SINCE 1948

Groceries, Fine Wine, Beer , Candy, Beach Supplies, Toys, Beachwear, Books and even Bike Rentals

Upstairs *"Gift Gallery"*

Open Daily | 252-986-2381

Located on **Highway** 12, on the way to the **Ferry Docks**

Lee Robinson's General Store

Hwy. 12,
Hatteras Village   (252) 986-2381

Lee Robinson's General Store, on the south end of Hatteras Village, has been serving the village since 1948, though it's in an old-looking new building now. It's a convenient place to stop for groceries, gourmet items, snacks, drinks, beer and fine wine, and ice. It's also a fun place to shop for books, maps, souvenirs and beach supplies. There's a neat gift gallery upstairs.

Farmer's Daughter

Hatteras Landing, Marina Way,
Hatteras Village   (252) 986-9970

The Farmer's Daughter, with several locations , offers coastal decor with a hint of country charm, plus garden decor and a variety of gifts and Outer Banks souvenirs. Choose from home accessories, local artwork, nautical gifts, carved birds, popular collectibles, afghans, prints, Christmas ornaments and more.

Kitty Hawk Kites/ Carolina Outdoors

Hatteras Landing, Marina Way,
Hatteras Village   (252) 986-1446

One of the Outer Banks' foremost recreation outfitters, Kitty Hawk Kites is the place to call to set up kayak ecotours on Hatteras Island (see the Recreation chapter). The store sells kites and other fun things, like flags, windsocks, toys, boomerangs and games. Carolina Outdoors is an outdoor-lifestyle outfitter, offering causal apparel, T-shirts, hats, sunglasses, sandals and more.

See **www.hatterasguide.com** for full content, links & updates.

FISHING • SHOPPING • DINING • LODGING

Austin Creek Baking Co. · Austin Creek Grill
Kitty Hawk Kites · Carolina Outdoors
Birthday Suits · Surfside Casuals
Farmer's Daughter · Graveyard Deli & Market
Sweet Sam's Cones & Cookies
Hatteras Landing Provision Co.
Hatteras Landing Marina

Residential Rental Units Available Late Summer 2005

www.hatteraslanding.com

Located beside the Hatteras/Ocracoke Ferry Dock

Birthday Suits
Hatteras Landing, Marina Way,
Hatteras Village   (252) 986-2282

Birthday Suits is the quintessential beach outfitter. They have a vast selection of swimsuits for men, women and children, including women's separates so you can find the perfect fit. Hard-to-fit bodies can find their swimsuit match here, and maternity and mastectomy suits are available. Birthday Suits also offers casual clothing for men and women, including all the official OBX gear and great accessories.

Surfside Casuals
Hatteras Landing, Marina Way,
Hatteras Village   (252) 986-2727

Surfside Casuals is an Outer Banks favorite for swimwear and casual clothing. You'll find clothing and T-shirts for men, women and children, plus sandals, accessories and OBX gear.

Hatteras Landing Provision Co.
Hatteras Landing, Marina Way,
Hatteras Village   (252) 986-2205

Lots of people run into this store while they wait in the ferry line to get to Ocracoke. They stock sweatshirts, T-shirts, hats and other clothing emblazoned with Outer Banks and Hatteras Island themes, plus a variety of other souvenirs and necessities, like film and sunglasses. The Graveyard Deli and Market is part of this store and offers deli sandwiches, snacks, candy, drinks, sundries and other things. 🦐

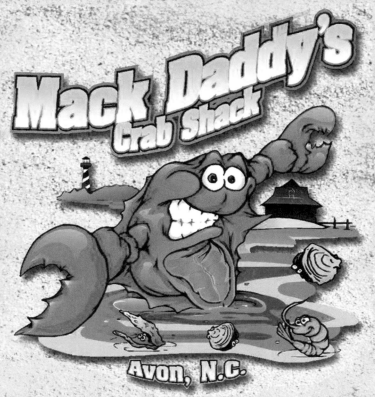

Hatteras Island Restaurants ❧

The best thing about dining out on Hatteras Island is that there are no chain restaurants (except Subway in Avon, but it's locally owned by great people) so everywhere you eat you can expect originality, personality, fresh ingredients and even some secret family recipes instead of predictable atmosphere and fare. All of the Hatteras Island restaurants reflect the laid-back personality of the island lifestyle in a variety of ways, but you can rest assured that the owners, chefs and staff are quite serious and very professional about the fare they serve and the experience they offer.

With fresh seafood brought to the local docks daily, most island restaurants put a major focus on the bounty of the sea. Local menus tout such specialties as Gulf Stream fish (yellowfin tuna, wahoo and mahi-mahi), inshore fish (trout, flounder and drum), succulent crab meat, oysters, clams, scallops, mussels and more. Restaurants will let you know what's in season, and therefore the freshest, when you're on the island. If it's soft-shell crabs, don't miss a chance to taste these delicacies! Fried seafood is no longer the staple of local menus, but you can get it if you want it. Most restaurants feature more healthy preparations, like steaming,

grilling, sautéing, blackening or broiling. If you want to cook seafood yourself, there are several seafood markets on the island; those are included in the listings in our Shopping chapter.

If you're not a seafood lover, don't worry. Even the seafood restaurants offer a wealth of other options, like beef, pasta, chicken, pork and vegetarian entrees. And not every restaurant on the island is seafood-oriented. You'll find down-home North Carolina barbecue, Italian and Chinese restaurants, plus pizza places, delis, ice cream shops and bakeries.

Meals are reasonably and fairly priced on Hatteras Island, and dress is very casual, even at the island's upscale restaurants. At this writing, Hatteras Island restaurants can only serve beer and wine. Most Hatteras Island restaurants close for some portion of the winter, though there is always something open, even in the dead of winter, to serve the growing population of locals. If you're dining out from November through March, it's best to call ahead to make sure your restaurant of choice is open. We have listed the island's restaurants geographically from north to south, starting in Rodanthe and ending in Hatteras Village.

Rodanthe, Waves & Salvo

Rose's Spot

Hwy. 12, Rodanthe   (252) 987-1315

Rose's Spot is in the little strip shopping center next to the Rodanthe Texaco. It's a casual spot, with seating indoors or out, and offers pizza, subs and sandwiches, appetizers, baskets and wings.

Marilyn's Deli

Island Convenience, Hwy. 12, Rodanthe   (252) 987-2239

There's a constant flow of customers at this convenience store deli counter, so you know that's a sign that the food is delicious. For lunch you can get soup, sandwiches, fried chicken, fries, deli meats and ice cream, and the service is quick. One hot meal is offered each day at lunch, something like roasted turkey or roast beef and vegetables. The deli also serves breakfast, including fresh-made biscuits and breakfast platters. This is a great place to pick up a quick meal and all the ice, drinks, tackle and supplies you'll need for a fishing trip or beach day.

Lisa's Pizzeria

Hwy. 12, Rodanthe   (252) 987-2525

Lisa's, celebrating its 21st year in 2005, is legendary on Hatteras Island. Come here for lunch or dinner to chow down on Italian favorites like hand-tossed pizza, calzones, lasagna, manicotti and spaghetti. Submarine sandwiches and burgers are also on the menu. The side dishes are excellent, including salads, fried mushrooms and broccoli, chicken wings and outstanding garlic cheese bread. Small and

casual, Lisa's is great for eating in, but they also offer take out and free delivery.

Boardwok South

Pamlico Station, Hwy. 12, Rodanthe   (252) 987-1080

Boardwok South brings something for the adventurous palates of Hatteras Island. Billing itself as an Asian-American eatery, it offers delicious Asian-style entrees from the wok, incorporating fresh vegetables, seafood, chicken, rice and noodles into flavorful, healthful dishes. There's also an Americanized side to the menu, with surf and turf entrees, sandwiches, kids' offerings and excellent sides. Boardwok South's atmosphere is clean, comfortably spartan and relaxing, with a full bar in back.

Tiki Grill

Hwy. 12, Rodanthe   (252) 987-1088

Tiki Grill is a fun-loving place that welcomes you as you are. Its laid-back style suits the surfing town of Rodanthe perfectly. It's lively and fun, and the fare is delicious. Choose from burgers, sandwiches, salads, seafood, entrees and some vegetarian offerings. Happy Hour and entertainment are held throughout the summer season. The staff at Tiki Grill takes a break on Sundays.

Leonardo's Pizza

Reef Store, Hwy. 12, Rodanthe
                           (252) 987-6522

Leonardo's offers delicious pizza with a variety of toppings, calzones and hearty subs stuffed with all the favorite fillings. It's located at the Reef beach supplies store in Rodanthe. You can pick up or have it delivered in Rodanthe, Waves or Salvo.

Top Dog Café

Hwy. 12, Waves   (252) 987-1272

For lunch or dinner, the Top Dog offers burgers, cheese steaks, steamed and fried seafood, salads, shrimp and oyster baskets, all-beef hot dogs, beer and wonderful appetizers. You can eat inside, on the screened porch or on the sound-view sundeck. This is a great place to take the whole family as there are special kids' offerings and the atmosphere is casual. Take-out is available.

Down Under Restaurant and Lounge

Hwy. 12, Waves   (252) 987-2277

Now in its 14th year, Down Under is a longtime favorite family restaurant on northern Hatteras Island. Adventurous eaters might want to try the Australian specialties, including kangaroo burgers and Aussie-inspired sandwiches. But Down Under is really known for its seafood. The menu also includes chicken, pasta, steaks and kids' offerings. The view of the sound and sunsets is fantastic, and large parties are welcome. It's open for lunch and dinner.

Island Pizza and Steam Bar

St. Waves Plaza, Hwy. 12,
Waves   (252) 987-2005

This restaurant in Waves offers just what the name says. The pizzas lean toward gourmet, with top-shelf ingredients, creative toppings and homemade crust. Sandwiches are available at lunch, and Italian pasta dishes are available at dinner. The steam bar features fresh shrimp, crab legs, clams, oysters and all the seafood favorites. Beer and wine available. Free delivery is available in the Tri-Village area, and there is a takeout window here.

See **www.hatterasguide.com** for full content, links & updates.

Avon

Blue Parrot Café
Waterside Shops, Hwy. 12,
Avon   (252) 995-6993

Some might say the sound view is the Blue Parrot's best attribute, but its laid-back atmosphere and chef-prepared fare are equally good. The food is simple and delicious. Choose from lots of sand-wiches, seafood, beef and chicken entrees, great daily specials, an extensive kids' menu and homemade desserts. Steamed shrimp specials are offered in the early afternoons, and breakfast and lunch are served in season and on weekends in the off season.

Dairy Queen
Hwy. 12, Avon   (252) 995-5624

You probably know what to expect from the Avon Dairy Queen. Stop here for delicious soft-serve ice cream, old-fashioned dip tops, Blizzards, sundaes, cool drinks and snacks.

Java Junction
Hwy. 12, Avon   (252) 995-7020

Finally! A coffee shop in Avon. Java Junction serves coffee and espresso drinks plus fruit drinks and smoothies. Muffins, scones and other bakery items are available, and they serve sandwiches in the summer. It's also an Internet café, with high-speed Internet access.

Dolphin Den
Hwy. 12, Avon   (252) 995-7717

The Dolphin Den is a big, family restaurant that specializes in locally caught seafood. Seafood entrees are served with the traditional accompaniments — cole slaw, cornbread and fries. Favorites include the coconut shrimp, crab cakes, fried and broiled seafood platters and seafood linguine served with salad and bread. Steaks, salads, sandwiches, she-crab soup, a variety of appetizers and home-made desserts round out the menu. The Dolphin Den's Key lime pie was chosen as the best in North Carolina by the Travel Guide Association, and you can try it for lunch and dinner every day.

The Froggy Dog Restaurant & Bar

Hwy. 12, Avon   (252) 995-4106

Avon's good old Froggy Dog is all new. New owners and a new chef have made lots of changes that will ensure the name Froggy Dog lives on in Avon for a long time to come. The Dog serves breakfast, lunch and dinner seven days a week. Breakfast features omelets, eggs, French toast, pancakes or lighter fare, plus hot, fresh donuts. For lunch try 6 oz. burgers, awesome sandwiches, creative salads, gourmet hot dogs and more. For dinner, feast on an array of appetizers, seafood, steaks, chicken and much more. Save room for dessert, including make-your-own s'mores. The Froggy Dog is also a fun late-night hangout, with a game room, karaoke and live music several times a week.

Subway

Hwy. 12, Avon   (252) 995-6881

Swing by Subway to pick up picnics for the beach or lunch for your fishing trip. You'll find all the usual Subway offerings – design-your-own subs on several types of fresh-baked bread, sandwiches, Atkins-friendly wraps and

See **www.hatterasguide.com** for full content, links & updates.

wine. A game room keeps all ages entertained here. It's open for dinner only, year round except for a few weeks in the middle of winter.

Hodad's Café
Hwy. 12, Avon   (252) 995-7866

Hodad's is a cool little joint that the surfing and wind-surfing crowds enjoy for its easy atmosphere and good eats. Come as you are for lunch or dinner. The appetizer menu is extensive with such diverse offerings as fried pickles with horseradish sauce, oven-baked Brie, conch fritters, hummus and rumaki. Burgers, veggie burgers, sandwiches, salads and Hatteras clam chowder are favorites for lunch. At dinner you can get any of the sandwiches plus seafood, meat and vegetarian entrees and pasta dishes.

Udder Delights Ice Cream
Hwy. 12, Avon   (252) 995-4563

Here's the place to fill up on treats in central Avon. Udder Delights, in the Outer Banks Realty building, offers Edy's ice cream, soft serve, floats, shakes, sundaes, shaved ice and drinks.

Nino's Pizza
Hwy. 12, Avon   (252) 995-5358

Come to this Hatteras Island favorite for homemade Italian specialties – pizza on hand-tossed dough, calzones, spaghetti, lasagna, subs, hamburgers, salads and pastas. Delivery is available in Avon. Nino's serves lunch and dinner.

The Pickled Palm
Hwy. 12, Avon (across from the Avon Pier)   (252) 995-3323

This new island restaurant comes from the same folks who run the popular Pickled Steamer down the road. The Pickled Palm features seafood and light Mediterranean fare, with more than 100 menu items and an eclectic special board. The menu includes such treats as baked Brie, blue-corn fried oysters, sweet potato crab cakes and other intriguing options. Ten-cent shrimp are offered every day from 3 to 6 p.m. The atmosphere is casual and family friendly. There are two 40-inch plasma TVs with sports trivia games for sports fans, yet there's still a predominantly dining atmosphere for those who just want to enjoy a relaxing meal. Lunch and dinner are served every day.

The Pickled Steamer
Hatteras Island Plaza, Hwy. 12, Avon   (252) 995-3602

Beach-restaurant fare tends to be predictable, but The Pickled Steamer's extensive menu has many things you won't find anywhere else. Flat Tops are open-face tortillas with a variety of toppings, plus there are dozens of wraps, salads and sandwiches, stuffed baked potatoes, pasta dishes, unique appetizers and more. The Pickled Steamer is known for its popular 10-cent shrimp specials from 3 to 6 p.m. every day. The atmosphere is lively with an open kitchen. They serve lunch and dinner.

Bubba's Too BBQ and Chicken
Hatteras Island Plaza, Hwy. 12, Avon   (252) 995-4385

If you've had enough seafood, head to Bubba's, where you can get hickory-smoked barbecued beef, pork and chicken. Sandwiches and dinner plates are available, and the traditional sides will make your mouth water. Catering and take

out are available, or you can eat in. Bubba's offers free delivery for large orders.

Chinatown Chinese Restaurant
Hatteras Island Plaza, Hwy. 12, Avon   (252) 995-0118

Specializing in Szechuan, Hunan and Cantonese fare, Chinatown offers all the Chinese favorites and then some. The menu is so long you'll have trouble making up your mind. You can't go wrong with daily specials. Lunch and dinner are offered, and you can eat in or take out.

Topper's Pizza and Pasta
Hatteras Island Plaza, Hwy. 12, Avon   (252) 995-3109

The name says it all. Topper's offers pizza with hand-tossed dough and homemade sauces, calzones, pasta entrees, subs, appetizers, salads and desserts. The atmosphere is warm and friendly; you'll want to hang out. There's a good selection of beer and wine. Lunch and dinner are served, and specials and offered daily.

Buxton

Uncle Eddy's Frozen Custard and 18-Hole Minigolf
Hwy. 12, Buxton   (252) 995-4059

This is a great place to stop after a visit to the lighthouse. Uncle Eddy's serves rich, delicious frozen custard. There are more than 50 homemade flavors, from the fruity Hatteras Sunrise to Rum Raisin.

Uncle Eddy's Frozen Custard
Over 50 Homemade Flavors that Change Daily!
Create and enjoy your own custom dessert
NO RULES • FREE SAMPLES

Relax and enjoy delicious Coffee creations!
Serving Expresso, Latte, Mocha and exotic
blends all in a unique laid back setting.

COFFEE

Buxton's only
18-hole
Miniature Golf
$2 Kids, $5 Adults
UNLIMITED
PLAY ALL DAY
OPEN DAILY
7 AM – 11 PM
995-4059

Angelo's Pizza and Buxton Drive In

Hwy. 12, Buxton
(252) 995-6364 (Angelo's)
(252) 995-6900 (Drive In)

If you all can't agree on where to eat, come here, where it's two restaurants in one. You order at one of two counters then all sit together in the big dining room. Angelo's offers pizza, subs, spaghetti, lasagna and other Italian favorites, while Buxton Drive In offers sandwiches, seafood baskets, shrimp burgers, cheeseburgers, barbecue and a great crab cake sandwich. To top it off, there's a huge game room (see Recreation).

Diamond Shoals Restaurant

Hwy. 12, Buxton   (252) 995-5217

Diamond Shoals is well known for its hearty breakfasts. Get here early for eggs, pancakes, bacon, sausage and all the delicious sides you'd expect. It's also a popular dinner spot, with steaks, seafood, pasta, a salad bar and chef's specials. Lunch, including seafood baskets, sandwiches and burgers, is served in season, between Memorial Day and Labor Day. Diamond Shoals is a family-style restaurant with a friendly staff and a welcoming atmosphere. Everyone loves the all-you-can-eat specials and the big saltwater aquariums, especially kids.

Finnegan's Dining Haul

Hwy. 12, Buxton   (252) 995-3060

Conveniently located across from the entrance to the lighthouse, Finnegan's serves lunch and dinner. The lunch menu features its signature U-boat sandwiches, burgers, pizza and a bunch of great appetizers (nachos, wings, conch fritters, onion rings and more). The dinner menu adds seafood, beef and other entrees. Beer and wine are offered. Finnegan's is open year round but is closed on Wednesdays in the off-season.

Tides Restaurant

Hwy. 12, Buxton   (252) 995-5988

A long-standing Hatteras Island favorite, Tides Restaurant is a good call for dinner. They specialize in the freshest local seafood available, but also offer steak, chicken and creative daily specials. Be sure to try the homemade desserts. Beer and wine are served, and Tides has its brown-bagging license if you want to bring your own spirits. This restaurant is completely smoke-free and handicapped accessible. The local artwork on the walls is for sale, so you just might go home with more than dinner. Reservations are not accepted. Tides is open nightly for dinner from April through November. The restaurant is not directly visible from N.C. 12. Look for the pelican on the restaurant sign, just across from the entrance to the Cape Hatteras Lighthouse.

Orange Blossom Bakery

Hwy. 12, Buxton   (252) 995-4109

The Orange Blossom is a Hatteras Island favorite for breakfast. Everyone loves the Apple Uglies, pastries, homemade biscuits, bagels, croissants and breakfast sandwiches. Breakfast is served from 7 until 11:30 a.m. Monday through Saturday, but the pastries can go fast so get there early. Orange Blossom also serves organic coffees and espresso. The little building that houses the bakery is more than 50 years old and was once the Orange Blossom Motel, named for orange trees that grew on the property.

Cool Wave Ice Cream Shoppe

Hwy. 12, Buxton   (252) 995-6366

This brightly painted shop in the fork of Back Road and N.C. 12 is a great place to stop for treats. The ice cream is excellent, and you can play a round of mini-golf while you're here.

Buoy's Restaurant

Osprey Shopping Center, Hwy. 12,
Buxton   (252) 995-6575

Buoy's Restaurant is open for lunch and dinner, and its large menu will please everyone in your crowd. It's a nice restaurant with an upscale atmosphere, but it's casual enough to bring the kids. Lunch features salads, soups, appetizers, seafood plates, lunch plates and sandwiches. At dinner there are more seafood entree offerings, steamed seafood, beef and chicken, house specials and a kids' menu. The salads are fresh and original, and the appetizers are imaginative. Beer and wine are available, and brown-bagging is permitted.

Buxton Munch Company

Osprey Shopping Center, Hwy. 12,
Buxton   (252) 995-5502

"Yum" is all we can say. Buxton Munch Company serves awesome eats. The wraps and quesadillas are stand outs, and the side dishes are so good it's hard

to choose. Soup, salads, munchies (beer-battered onion rings, egg rolls, wings), sandwiches, burgers, salads, seafood baskets, fried chicken and specials are offered for lunch and dinner, take out or eat in. Eating in is fun because this place is lively, the background music is good and the people are friendly.

The Pilot House

Hwy. 12, Buxton   (252) 995-5664

If you're expecting a fabulous view with your meal – and who wouldn't on Hatteras Island? – The Pilot House offers panoramic vistas of Pamlico Sound. It's a popular dinner spot, especially around sunset. If you have to wait for a table, kick back on the deck or in the bar with a beer or glass of fine wine and enjoy the view. The Pilot House serves dinner only, offering up fresh, Southern-style seafood, steaks, pasta, vegetarian dishes, nightly specials, a kids' menu and killer desserts. Brown-bagging is allowed.

Fish House Restaurant

Hwy. 12, Buxton   (252) 995-5151

As far as fish houses go, this is the real thing — a former fish house right on Buxton Harbor, where fishing boats unload their catches. The restaurant is incredibly charming, with sloping floors, fabulous harbor and water views, a mark on the wall from the last flood,

and dining right on the dock. Steamed seafood is a specialty (with hush puppies and veggies on the side), though landlubber entrees are available too. You can get pasta or steak entrees or choose from the daily specials. Lunch and dinner are served at this casual place.

Pop's Raw Bar

Hwy. 12, Buxton   (252) 995-7734

Pop's is frequented by a lot of locals – a sign that the seafood meets local standards of excellence. Across from Buxton Harbor, Pop's specializes in steamed seafood, including shrimp, clams, oysters and crab legs. They also have more hearty fare, like burgers, subs, barbecue, seafood platters and a lot more. They're open for lunch and dinner, and they close on Sundays.

Sandbar and Grill

Hwy. 12, Buxton   (252) 995-3413

The Sandbar is an island favorite with a view of Pamlico Sound that can't be beat. The menu includes homemade soup, specials, great appetizers, steamed seafood, sandwiches, burgers, ribs, pasta, seafood entrees and children's offerings. It's open for lunch and dinner and is also one of the few late-night spots on the island. Live music, karaoke, NTN trivia, Foosball, pool tables and a late-night menu will please all the night owls.

Frisco

Gingerbread House Bakery

Hwy. 12, Frisco   (252) 995-5204

The Gingerbread House Bakery is famous for its baked goods and specialty pizzas. Open in the evenings only, they

See www.hatterasguide.com for full content, links & updates.

desserts are irresistible. The bakery is closed on Sunday and Monday.

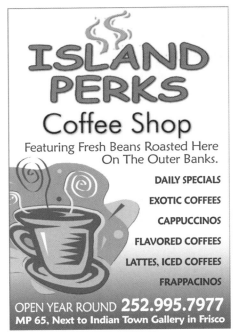

Island Perks Coffee Shop

Hwy. 12, Frisco   (252) 995-7977

Used to be if you wanted a quick cup of coffee on Hatteras Island you had to hit a convenience store. But no more! Hatteras now has real coffee options, and even quiet Frisco is part of the coffee culture. Island Perks offers expertly made espresso and coffee drinks, including cappuccino, lattes, mochas and more, plus delicious chai. They use locally roasted beans so they're always fresh. Sweets and pastries are available too. It's open seven days a week, starting at 7 am. Island Perks shares space with Indian Town Gallery, which is coffee friendly, so you can sip your coffee while you browse among fine art.

offer pizza on delicious homemade crust with a mind-boggling array of toppings. Pizza is available for take out as well. A salad bar with fresh veggies rounds out the dinner offerings. The homemade cookies, brownies, gingerbread and other

Bubba's BBQ

Hwy. 12, Frisco   (252) 995-5421

Bubba's hickory-smoked barbecue has had a loyal following for more than 20 years. Maybe it's because of Bubba's original sauce, or maybe it's the way they slow-cook

Photo Courtesy: Elaine Danis

Bar-B-Q in Frisco . . . everyone loves it.

See **www.hatterasguide.com** for full content, links & updates.

the ribs, pork, beef, turkey and chicken. The fried chicken is also a hit. Be sure to save room for homemade dessert. Eat in, carry out and catering are available. Delivery is offered for large orders.

Quarterdeck Restaurant

Hwy. 12, Frisco   (252) 986-2425
    Established in 1978, the Quarterdeck has been serving Hatteras Islanders for nearly a quarter of a century. This is a locally owned, casual, family-oriented restaurant specializing in seafood (try the crab cakes and stuffed flounder), char-grilled steaks and homemade desserts. A kids' menu, beer and wine are available.

Hatteras Village

Fish Tales

Hwy. 12, Hatteras Village
(252) 986-6516   (252) 986-6518
    Fish Tales is a family-friendly restaurant in a bright pink building on the very north end of Hatteras. The menu is varied enough that you could eat all three meals here every day and try something new every time. For breakfast, try the omelets, French toast or incredible variety of pancakes. Breakfast is served until noon for late risers. Come back for lunch for great appetizers, salads, seafood sandwiches, burgers, subs and ruebens. At dinner time, come in for appetizers, soups, salad, seafood platters, meat entrees and pasta. A kids' menu is offered. Beer and wine are available, and you can order carry-out from the full menu. Breakfast and lunch are served every day, and dinner is served five nights a week.

Rocco's Pizza

Hwy. 12, Hatteras Village
                    (252) 986-2150
    Newly redecorated thanks to Hurricane Isabel, Rocco's is the place in Hatteras Village for pizza and Italian dishes. For lunch or dinner you can order Italian specialties, pizza, subs, salads and even some seafood. This is a casual, family-oriented restaurant with delicious food.

The Hatterasman and the Hatteras Sushi Co.

Hwy. 12, Hatteras Village
                    (252) 986-1001
    For great eats, the Hatterasman can't be beat. Open for lunch and dinner, the casual restaurant specializes in quick and delicious food like burgers, tacos, burritos, sandwiches and a great variety of sides and appetizers. A new element of the

Channel Bass Restaurant
TRADITIONAL HATTERAS STYLE
FAMILY DINING
Fresh Local Seafood, Fresh Cut Steaks
Wine and Beer, Brown Bagging
Closed Sundays   *Little Hatteras* **252.986.2250**   Est. 1965

Hatterasman is the Hatteras Sushi Co., featuring rolls, sashimi and appetizers. Sushi is available at dinner only.

Channel Bass Restaurant
Hwy. 12, Hatteras Village
(252) 986-2250

The Channel Bass has been serving dinner to Hatteras Villagers since 1965. This super-casual restaurant is known for its preparations of the fresh local seafood. Menu favorites are the Seafood Delight,

the homemade crab imperial, crab cakes and steamed seafood platters. Everyone loves the hot, fresh hushpuppies. Channel Bass also serves chicken, burgers, sandwiches, steaks and nightly specials, including rib and veal specials. A children's menu is available. Beer and wine are served, and brown-bagging is allowed.

The Dancing Turtle Coffee Shop
Hwy. 12, Hatteras Village
(252) 986-4004

The coffee-shop craze has finally hit Hatteras Island. The Dancing Turtle is the real deal, with espresso, lattes, mochas, cappuccinos and just plain wonderful coffee. They also serve fruit smoothies, chai, frozen drinks, organic teas, baked goods and biscotti. The atmosphere is warm and friendly; hang around awhile and meet some of the regulars. Pottery and gifts are for sale. It's open year round.

Breakwater Restaurant
Hwy. 12 at Oden's Dock,
Hatteras Village   (252) 986-2733

The Breakwater at Oden's Dock is a locals' favorite, and visitors are known to make many repeat visits as well. The second-story restaurant and bar overlook the harbor and its stone breakwater, from which the restaurant gets its name. The

See **www.hatterasguide.com** for full content, links & updates.

The
Dancing Turtle
coffee shop

Espresso
Smoothies
Good Times

Located in Hatteras Village   Open All Year   986-4004

view of the sound and the sunsets is breathtaking. The restaurant serves dinner only, with a menu featuring creative, contemporary preparations of seafood, prime rib and other meats, and pasta. The fresh-baked bread and desserts are delicious. The atmosphere is sophisticated yet casual and family friendly. Live acoustic entertainment is offered on the deck on some summer evenings. Be sure to check out the old photos of Hatteras Village on the dining room walls.

Dinky's

Village Marina, Hwy. 12,
Hatteras Village   (252) 986-2020

Dinky's is a new restaurant in Hatteras Village, opened in February 2005. Its name stems from the fact that the folks at the Village Marina call their small marina the "best dink marina in town." This is a small, 40-seat restaurant but it has a great big view. The restaurant is on the second level of the marina, and the view of the sound is panoramic and unobstructed. At

Photo Courtesy: Elaine Danis

Friendly service, varied menus and quality fresh ingredients characterize the islands' most popular eating establishments.

See **www.hatterasguide.com** for full content, links & updates.

sunset, make time to sit at the beautiful African mahogany bar with a cold beer before dinner. Dinky's serves dinner only for now, but they may add lunch in season. The fare is American traditional, with seafood, steaks, chicken, appetizers and lots of creative specials. Families are welcome. Everything is available for take-out.

Harbor Delicatessen

Hatteras Harbor Marina, Hwy. 12, Hatteras Village   (252) 986-2552

The Harbor Delicatessen at Hatteras Harbor Marina offers breakfast, lunch and take-out fare. It's a great place to pick up lunches for a fishing trip. Breakfast includes biscuit and bagel sandwiches. The lunch menu is large, with lots of specialty sandwiches, cold-cut sandwiches, burgers,

Photo Courtesy: Elaine Danis

Fresh seafood, good friends, classic dishes and Southern hospitality. That's Hatteras dining.

See **www.hatterasguide.com** for full content, links & updates.

seafood salads, daily specials and sides. It opens at 6 a.m. year round and stays open until 6 p.m. in the summer months.

Sonny's Restaurant
Hwy. 12, Hatteras Village
(252) 986-2922

Serving Hatteras for more than 28 years, Sonny's serves breakfast and dinner. Breakfast is rib-sticking, with omelets, pancakes, homemade biscuits and sausage gravy. Dinner features nightly specials, fresh seafood platters, hand-cut steaks, pasta and fabulous mixed grills. Steamer specials include Dungeness crab, Alaskan snow crab legs, shrimp, crawfish, mussels and clams. Sonny's closes in the off-season.

Teach's Island Bar and Grill
Teach's Lair Marina, Hwy. 12, Hatteras Village

Here's another new restaurant in Hatteras Village for 2005. Teach's Island is located at Teach's Lair Marina right by the water with a great view of the boats, the sound and the sunsets. The restaurant is Hatteras-style, which means it's casual and fun. The atmosphere is relaxed and the fare is simple and light: burgers, fish and crab cake sandwiches, steamed shrimp and seafood, wings, seafood baskets and some Mexican specialties. Lunch and dinner are served year round, and the bar offers beer and wine. Families are welcome.

Graveyard Deli and Market
Hatteras Landing, Marina Way, Hatteras Village   (252) 986-2205

Part of the Hatteras Landing Provision Company, this deli offers light

breakfast fare, hot dogs, sandwiches, subs and wraps to take out or eat on the porch. It's right next to the Ocracoke ferry docks, and many people waiting in the ferry line grab a quick lunch or snack here. The market has all the chips, snacks, candy and drinks you need to go along with your sandwich.

Austin Creek Baking Company
Hatteras Landing, Marina Way, Hatteras Village   (252) 986-1578

An artisan bakery on Hatteras Island? Yes, it's true. This is the place to find irresistible pastries, desserts and breads – all baked fresh every day. The coffee is excellent too. You can also get a great lunch here, from sandwiches on fresh-baked bread to stone-oven pizza. Austin Creek bakes desserts for special occasions

served in a

Spectacular

DOCKSIDE SETTING

AUSTIN CREEK GRILL

a waterfront bistro • Hatteras Landing

**Fresh Local Seafood
Contemporary Southern Cusine
Fine Wines and Beer**

252.986.1511

**austin creek
baking company**

grains, beans, pastries & pizza

**Gourmet Coffees & Breakfast Bakeries
Sweet Treats Pastries Cakes Cookies
Pizzas Calzones Specialty Sandwiches**

252.986.1578

**SWEET SAM'S
CONES & COOKIES**

**Gourmet Ice Cream
Fresh Baked Cookies**

next to the ferry docks Hatteras Landing
www.hatteraslanding.com/austincreekgrill

if you call ahead. It's open daily in season; call for off-season hours. The bakery closes in January.

Austin Creek Grill

Hatteras Landing, Marina Way,
Hatteras Village   (252) 986-1511

Austin Creek Grill is upscale though casual and inviting. It's right on the docks at Hatteras Landing, so you can dine with a view of the boats in the harbor and the water. The Culinary Institute of America–trained chef specializes in creative preparations of local seafood and fish (he'll even cook your own catch) and contemporary Southern cuisine. The wine list is carefully selected to match the fare, and the desserts are delectable. It's open nightly in season; call for off-season hours. The restaurant closes in January.

Hatteras Island Accommodations ❧

atteras Island offers a wide variety of accommodations, so there is something to suit everyone. The island has about a dozen classic, old-school motels, some of which have been serving vacationers since the 1950s and '60s. These motels are clean and comfortable and updated with new amenities, but they are infused with the flavor of old Hatteras Island. These basic accommodations are favored by fishermen, families on a budget and people who long for the simplicity of yesteryear. You can expect to find a range of amenities in the island's hotels and motels, including one chain hotel in Buxton and a few bed-and-breakfast inns.

Camping is big on Hatteras Island. There are more than a dozen campgrounds dotting the island, from simple mom-and-pop establishments to camping mega-resorts. Tent or trailer campers looking to get back to nature will enjoy the no-frills National Park Service campgrounds at Buxton and Frisco or some of the smaller campgrounds. RV travelers seeking full hookups, swimming pools, game rooms, planned activities and the camaraderie of the RV lifestyle will not be disappointed with the island's camping resorts.

The most popular form of island accommodation is the rental home, in which vacationers rent a fully equipped house by the week. There are thousands of rental homes on Hatteras Island, ranging from two bedrooms on the sound to 10 or more bedrooms on the oceanfront, some luxurious, some simple. Rental home prices vary according to their amenities and proximity to the water. The rental process is made easy by several professional property management companies who take care of everything from deposits and contracts to cleaning and maintenance. Rental homes are generally only available by the week, though you may be able to get a partial week in the off-season. For late summer and fall rentals, the rental company will typically offer you the option of hurricane insurance for renters. It doesn't cost much, and if you purchase it you won't lose a deposit or be out any money if a hurricane threatens during your rental week.

All three types of accommodations are available on Hatteras Island year

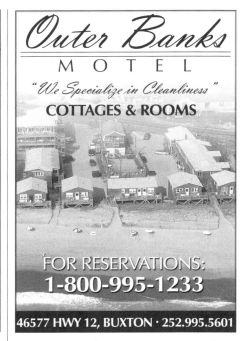
round, though some establishments close in the winter. The summer season is when rates are at their highest because that is when there is most demand for accommodations. Be sure to make reservations well in advance. Fall is also a busy season on Hatteras Island because of the excellent fishing.

The accommodations in this chapter are organized into three categories: Hotels and Motels, Campgrounds, and Vacation Rentals. Within these categories, the accommodations options are listed in geographical order from north to south, starting in Rodanthe and ending in Hatteras Village.

Hotels & Motels
Rodanthe-Waves-Salvo

Sea Sound Motel
Sea Sound Rd.,
Rodanthe   (252) 987-2224

Sea Sound Motel is located mid-island, between Highway 12 and the ocean, though the beach is only a five-minute walk away. There are 11 rooms here, including efficiencies with full kitchenettes, deluxe rooms with two queens with mini-kitchens and regular rooms with one queen bed. A swimming pool is on site, plus there's a picnic area and fish-cleaning station.

Salvo Inn Motel

Hwy. 12, Salvo   (252) 987-2240

The only motel in Salvo offers basic accommodations just a short walk from the ocean. The Salvo Inn Motel has 16 rooms, three of which are efficiencies. All rooms have a microwave oven, refrigerator and coffeemaker. The motel also has three rental cottages . One is a three-bedroom, and the others have two bedrooms.

Avon

Avon Motel

Hwy. 12, Avon   (252) 995-5774

This old-school beach motel offers nearly 50 clean, comfortable standard motel rooms and efficiency apartments. Rooms have outside entry, so you can park by your door. Ocean access and a fish-cleaning station are offered. The motel is located at the northern stoplight at the corner of N.C. 12 and Harbor Drive.

Buxton

Inn on Pamlico Sound

Hwy. 12, Buxton
(252) 995-7030   (800) PAMLICO

The Inn on Pamlico Sound is a casually elegant 12-room bed and breakfast located right on the banks of the Pamlico Sound. Accommodations range from garden-view queens to premium sound-front kings with private porches and two-person whirlpool baths. Amenities include a three-course gourmet breakfast every morning, fresh baked goods every afternoon, kayaks, bicycles, a sound-front pool, a 14-seat state-of-the-art home theater, a print library, an 1,100-title DVD collection, complimentary beverages and snacks, beach chairs, beach towels, and high-speed Internet access in every room. It's located in a quiet, peaceful section of Buxton just north of the Frisco line.

Cape Hatteras Motel

Hwy. 12, Buxton
(252) 995-5611   (800) 995-0711

The Cape Hatteras Motel offers 39 rooms including 27 on the oceanfront and 12 on the soundside. The motel offers standard rooms with a microwave, refrigerator and coffeemaker in the room and efficiency apartments and townhouses with full kitchens. A swimming pool, hot tub and cable TV are offered, but phones are not available in the rooms. They are open year round.

Outer Banks Motel

Hwy. 12, Buxton
(252) 995-5601   (800) 995-1233

On the oceanfront in north Buxton, Outer Banks Motel offers 10 standard

rooms, six efficiencies with full kitchens and 13 cottages, all with phones and cable TV. The motel has a pool, library and rowboats for guest use. The cottages and efficiencies are available by the week only in the summer, but the standard rooms are available by the night. Outer Banks Motel also offers 20 cottages in the heart of Buxton, about a mile back from the ocean. These cottages range from one to three bedrooms and rent by the night or week.

Lighthouse View Motel
Hwy. 12, Buxton   (252) 995-5680

The Lighthouse View Motel offers 24 standard motel rooms sleeping two to four, 26 efficiency apartments with kitchens, and 28 cottages ranging from two to four bedrooms and sleeping six to 10 people. All rooms and cottages are on the oceanside in north Buxton. Some rooms have ocean views, while others face the sound. The motel has a heated outdoor pool and hot tub plus a lighted fish-cleaning table. They are open year round.

Comfort Inn of Hatteras Island
Hwy. 12, Buxton   (252) 995-6100

In a new building built to look like an old life-saving station, the Comfort Inn is one of Hatteras Island's newest accommodations options. There are 60 rooms here, each with a small refrigerator, microwave and coffeemaker. Rooms feature two doubles or one king, and some have a sleeper sofa. There's an outdoor pool as well. The office is open 24 hours, and the hotel is open year round.

46854 Hwy 12,
Buxton,
NC 27920

est. 1962

"Southern Hospitality Since 1962"
Chris & Tracy Lata
252-995-5968   800-635-6911
www.falconmotel.com

Falcon Motel

Hwy. 12, Buxton
(252) 995-5968   (800) 635-6911

Serving Hatteras Island for more than 40 years, this motel reminds us of a classic Florida motor inn, with neat landscaping and lots of trees, fresh coats of pastel paint on the buildings, door-side parking and a pool. It's on the soundside of the island, and there's a place where you can launch a kayak or canoe into the sound. A fish-cleaning table, complimentary bikes and picnic tables are available. The motel has 35 rooms, including five pet rooms, two apartments, three efficiencies with kitchenettes and two apartments with full kitchens.

Cape Pines Motel

Hwy. 12, Buxton   (252) 995-5666

Cape Pines Motel has been in operation since 1953. The motel has 29 rooms, three of which are one to two-bedroom suites with full kitchens. Standard rooms are the most affordable, while deluxe rooms have refrigerators, microwaves and coffeemakers. All rooms have cable TV but no phones. Cape Pines has a pool, grills, picnic tables, a fish-cleaning station, an outdoor shower and pay phone, and there's a fitness center next door. Guests can use the Internet during office hours.

Cape Hatteras B&B

Old Lighthouse Rd., Buxton
(252) 995-6004   (800) 252-3316

For B&B aficionados, this 13-year-old inn offers a true bed-and-breakfast experience in the casual beach town of Buxton. A full, home-cooked, hot breakfast is served to guests each morning. The inn has nine rooms in all, with a mix of double, queen and king beds, and a TV in each room. Public areas include a nice deck with a gas grill, tables and chairs. The inn is about 500 feet from the beach, and bicycles and beach chairs are available for guests to use.

Buxton Beach Motel

Old Lighthouse Rd.,
Buxton   (252) 995-5972

For those who love the charm of historic Hatteras Island, the Buxton Beach Motel offers simple, basic accommodations in one of the island's original motels — the way things used to be. This ground-level motel is clean and comfortable and offers 14 standard motel rooms, a few small cottages and two rental houses. Rooms have refrigerators, microwaves, cable TV, air-conditioning and heat. Pets are allowed for a fee, and the motel is just a short walk from the beach. Stop by and meet the friendly owners of this family owned and operated motel.

See **www.hatterasguide.com** for full content, links & updates.

Tower Circle Motel

Old Lighthouse Rd.,
Buxton   (252) 995-5353

On the island since 1956, the Tower Circle Motel offers a taste of old Hatteras Island in an updated atmosphere. There are 19 rooms here, consisting of one- and two-room efficiency apartments, eight large duplex apartments and standard rooms. All rooms have air-conditioning, heat and cable TV. There's a playground, fish-cleaning bench and pay phone onsite. The motel is very close to the beach and has ocean access.

Hatteras Village

Sea Gull Motel

Hwy. 12,
Hatteras Village   (252) 986-2550

The only oceanfront motel in Hatteras Village, the Sea Gull offers fantastic views and unbeatable access to the beach. The older building, resurrected after Hurricane Isabel, has 11 standard rooms (10 with two double beds and one with a king bed) with a microwave and a refrigerator. There are also three efficiencies with queen-size beds and full kitchens and one two-bedroom apartment with a full kitchen. High-speed Internet access is a bonus in every room. Complimentary coffee is offered in the office each morning. New in 2005 will be an outdoor pool plus a new building with four two-bedroom and two one-bedroom apartments.

Breakwater Inn

(formerly Hatteras Harbor Motel)

Hwy. 12,
Hatteras Village   (252) 986-2565

The Breakwater Inn is conveniently

located amongst the action of Hatteras Harbor, next to Oden's Dock, so it's a great place to stay if you're catching an early morning fishing charter. New in 2005 is a soundfront addition to the hotel, with 35 units, 23 of them with a water view. The older part of the hotel has 12 rooms, which were recently remodeled. All the rooms have microwaves, refrigerators, cable TV and a phone. There's high-speed Internet service in the office, an outdoor pool on site and fish-cleaning facilities next door at Oden's.

Village Marina Motel
Hwy. 12,
Hatteras Village   (252) 986-2522
The Village Marina Motel has risen from the ashes of Isabel with a new 12-room motel. The rooms have living areas and bedrooms with TVs, small refrigerators, microwaves, coffeemakers and

toasters. The motel is right on the harbor and offers the amenities of the marina and boat slips plus a fish-cleaning station.

Harbor View Apartments
Hwy. 12, Hatteras Village
(252) 986-2166   (800) 676-4939
Hatteras Harbor Marina rents apartments on the second floor of the marina building. The apartments overlook the harbor and Pamlico Sound and are available to rent by the night or week. The units have balconies, a full-size kitchen with microwave and coffeemaker, air conditioning, cable TV, linens and dishes. Apartments with an extra bedroom sleep up to six people.

Burrus Motor Court
Hwy. 12,
Hatteras Village   (252) 986-2363

Burrus Motor Court is on Highway 12, just across from Hatteras Harbor, making it the perfect accommodation for anglers taking charters from one of the Hatteras marinas. The motel offers standard rooms and efficiencies, with TVs in each room. There is a pool on site.

Hatteras Marlin Motel
Hwy. 12,
Hatteras Village   (252) 986-2141

Completely remodeled in 2004, the Hatteras Marlin Motel is like new. The motel has 39 units, including standard rooms, efficiencies and suites that sleep up to six people. All rooms have a refrigerator, microwave and coffeemaker, and the suites have a separate kitchen area. The

Hatteras Marlin Motel has an outdoor pool for in-season swimming, and it's only a mile from the beach. It's right in the heart of the village, close to restaurants, shops and the marinas.

The Villas at Hatteras Landing
Hwy. 12,
Hatteras Village   (800) 527-2903

This former Holiday Inn Express has been revamped into condominiums. The location can't be beat, next to the Hatteras Landing complex of fine dining, shopping and recreation and close to the beach, the Graveyard of the Atlantic Museum and the Ocracoke ferry docks. The Villas offers 53 upscale condominium suites, each with one bedroom, one bath, a full kitchen and a private balcony. There's a pool on site. These accommodations rent nightly or weekly.

See www.hatterasguide.com for full content, links & updates.

Camping

North Beach Campground
Hwy. 12, Rodanthe   (252) 987-2378

The North Beach Campground is on the oceanfront, which makes it quite popular. Most of the sites are rented permanently, and there's a waiting list for those sites. There are a few transient sites for tents and pull-through RVs and campers. Water and electricity are offered at every site. The bathhouse has hot and cold showers, and there's a Laundromat and small pool. The campground is behind the gas station, which sells groceries and RV supplies.

Rodanthe Watersports and Campground
Hwy. 12, Rodanthe   (252) 987-1431

Watersports enthusiasts love staying at this soundfront campground, where they can windsurf or kayak right from their RV or tent site and get discounts on renting the sports equipment. Electric and water hookups are available, and there's a full bathhouse with hot showers. It's within walking distance of the ocean, pier, convenience stores and restaurants.

Camp Hatteras
Hwy. 12, Waves   (252) 987-2777

Camp Hatteras is a sprawling 50-acre campground with both ocean and sound frontage and more than 300 sites. Every amenity you could possibly want is available, including full hookups, laundry facilities, bathhouses with hot showers, three swimming pools, hot tub, a clubhouse, tennis courts, miniature golf, water sports gear and more. Camp Hatteras is clean and well-kept, and it's open year round.

St. Clair Landing Campground
25028 Hwy. 12,
Rodanthe   (252) 987-2850

If you crave peace and quiet away from the masses, try this small soundfront campground. There are four hookup sites for RVs or campers, plus several primitive sites. The atmosphere is very casual and family-oriented. Hot showers and a bathhouse are offered.

Cape Hatteras KOA
Hwy. 12, Waves   (252) 987-2307

On the oceanfront, Cape Hatteras KOA has more than 300 campsites, plus small one- and two-room units known as Kamping Kabins. Campers are offered hot showers, bathhouses, laundry facilities,

CAPE WOODS CAMPGROUND & CABINS
Good Sampark
WOODALL'S RATED
252-995-5850
Fax: 252-995-3732
47649 Buxton Back Road
P.O. Box 690 • Buxton, NC 27920
www.capewoods.com

two pools, a hot tub, a general store, a café, a game room, miniature golf, kayak and paddle boat rentals, ocean access and recreational programs. The KOA is open March through December. They do accept campers year round with reservations, though there are limited amenities.

Ocean Waves Campground

Hwy. 12, Waves   (252) 987-2556

Ocean Waves offers around 68 spaces for RVs and tents. Each site has its own picnic table, and full hookups are available. There are three bathhouses, hot showers and laundry facilities. Campers also enjoy the game room, beach access and outdoor pool.

Sands of Time Campground

North End Rd., Avon   (252) 995-5596

This campground is tucked back in the quiet residential district of old Avon, but still it's not very far from the beach. Sands of Time offers full hookup sites that include water, electric, sewer and cable TV. Campers or motor homes up to 40 feet can be accommodated. There are 60 sites including a few tent sites. Hot showers, laundry facilities, picnic tables, a community fire ring and horseshoes are offered. To get here, head west on Harbor Road (at the north stoplight) then take a right on North End Road.

NPS Cape Point Campground

Near Cape Hatteras Lighthouse
(252) 473-2111

One of four National Park Service campgrounds within Cape Hatteras National Seashore, Cape Point Campground is on the oceanfront near Cape Hatteras Lighthouse Historic Site and Cape Hatteras. This is a popular camping spot, situated as it is near awesome fishing and recreational grounds. You can walk to the beach, lighthouse, the Buxton Woods Nature Trail and the village shops and restaurants. The NPS campgrounds accommodate both tents and RVs on 202 sites with no hookups. Each site has a grill, picnic table and parking pad. Restrooms, unheated showers, potable water, a recycling center, a pay phone and a dump station are available to campers. Reservations are not taken, so sites are assigned on a first-come, first-served basis. Pets are allowed if they're kept on a leash.

Island Hide-A-Way Campground

Buxton Back Rd.,
Buxton   (252) 995-6628

Nestled back in the quiet part of Buxton on the Back Road, Island Hide-A-Way is perfect for a little R&R. There are

24 full hookup sites, six partial hookup and numerous wooded tent sites. The bathhouses have hot and cold showers. A washer and dryer are available for guest use. Pets are welcome. Island Hide-A-Way is conveniently located in Buxton; Connor's grocery, an ice cream shop and a bank are nearby.

Cape Woods Campground
Buxton Back Rd.,
Buxton   (252) 995-5850
This family-owned campground is tucked back in the trees on Buxton Back Road, perfect for enjoying the solitude the island can offer. Cape Woods offers 130 sites, some for tents, others with full or partial hook-up, and cabins. You can rent nightly, monthly or seasonally, and pets on leashes are welcome. The site offers a pool, playground, game room, hot showers, heated bathhouses, laundry facilities, a security gate, fish-cleaning stations and a picnic pavilion.

NPS Frisco Campground
Off Hwy. 12,
Frisco   (252) 473-2111
Another of the four National Park Service campgrounds, Frisco Campground is like a well-kept secret. It is the quietest, most secluded of all the NPS camping areas and even has some trees and scrubby brush that give your site a little privacy. The campground is on the oceanfront, tucked safely behind a row of dunes. There are 127 sites here for tents and RVs, but there are no hookups. Each site has a grill, picnic table and parking pad, and restrooms, unheated showers and potable water are available to campers. Pets are allowed if they're on a leash. Reservations are not taken, so sites are

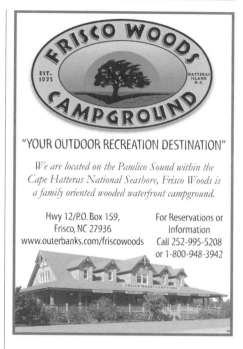

assigned on a first-come, first-served basis.

Frisco Woods Campground
Hwy. 12, Frisco
(252) 995-5208   (800) 948-3942
This campground is situated in the midst of Frisco Woods, so it offers nice shady shelter. The campground offers waterfront camping on Pamlico Sound, making it quite popular with visiting kite boarders and windsurfers. Full hookups are offered, and there's a dish-washing area, coin laundry, fish-cleaning bench, solar-heated swimming pool, bathhouses with hot showers, sound beach and huge store with gas, camping supplies, food and gifts. One- and two-room camping cabins feature air conditioning, outside water, grills and picnic tables.

Village Marina and Campground

Hwy. 12,
Hatteras Village   (252) 986-2522

Village Marina's campground is at the harbor, offering spectacular views of the harbor, sound and sunsets. There are 35 camper and RV sites. A bathhouse with hot showers and full hookups are available, and a restaurant is on site.

Hatteras Sands Campground

Eagle Pass Rd.,
Hatteras Village   (252) 986-2422

Hatteras Sands is off the beaten path of Highway 12, so it affords a feeling of relative seclusion. This Good Sam campground offers 102 sites, both tent and full hookup. Six colorful, two-room primitive cabins are also available. There are plenty of amenities to keep campers entertained, including a pool, hot tub, game room, snack bar, playground, paddle boats and pedal cars. Laundry facilities and two bathhouses are available.

Vacation Rentals

Avon Cottages

Hwy. 12, Avon   (252) 995-4123

Avon Cottages offers eight oceanfront cottages, seven semi-oceanfront cottages and 11 oceanside cottages. These modern rental homes greatly range in size, sleeping from 5 to 14. Each cottage has an ocean view, large living/dining/kitchen areas, central heat and air and is fully furnished. Some have Jacuzzis or hot tubs. The cottages are available to rent weekly, but there are also efficiency apartments available to rent by the night.

See **www.hatterasguide.com** for full content, links & updates.

Colony Realty

Hwy. 12, Avon
(252) 995-5891   (800) 962-5256
Hwy. 12, Hatteras   (252) 986-2350

Colony Realty rents houses, duplexes and condominiums in Avon, Buxton, Frisco and Hatteras Village. They also offer long-term rentals all over the island. There's a range of offerings, from a cozy two-bedroom cottage in Avon to a six-bedroom mega-house on the oceanfront.

Dolphin Realty

Hwy. 12, Hatteras Village
(252) 986-2241   (800) 338-4775

Dolphin Realty rents condominiums and cottages from Avon to Hatteras Village. Homes range across the island, from oceanfront to soundfront.

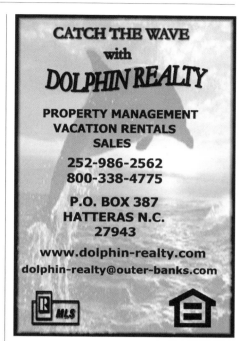

See **www.hatterasguide.com** for full content, links & updates.

Hatteras Realty

Hwy. 12, Avon   (252) 995-5466
Hwy. 12, Hatteras Village
(252) 995-5466   (800) HATTERAS

Hatteras Realty represents about 475 properties from Avon to Hatteras Village. Their rental homes range from three bedrooms to 10 bedrooms, oceanfront and soundfront, and they have some special properties that can accommodate weddings, reunions or retreats.

All renters are allowed access to the Club Hatteras in Avon, which includes an enormous heated pool, showers and changing area, beach access, tennis courts and putting greens.

Club Hatteras also has high-tech conference and meeting facilities and areas that can be used for events like wedding receptions. Hatteras Realty offers fee-based programs for kids and adults. In summer, the Kinnakeet Sound Adventure day camp for children and a Kids' Night Out on Tuesday nights give kids a fun break from their parents. Adults can take seafood cooking classes on Wednesday nights, and the whole family will enjoy "Storms and Shipwrecks," a one-man play, on Thursday nights.

Midgett Realty

Hwy. 12, Rodanthe   (252) 987-2350
Island Shops, Hwy. 12,
Avon   (252) 995-5333
Hwy. 12, Hatteras
(252) 986-2841   (800) 527-2903

The Midgetts are a native family who were the first to offer vacation rentals on Hatteras Island. They offer approximately 550 rental homes and are well represented

in all seven villages. Homes range from modest cottages for fishermen to luxury palaces for big families. Midgett also represents the condominiums at The Villas at Hatteras Landing.

Outer Beaches Realty

Hwy. 12, Waves   (252) 987-2771
Hwy. 12, Avon   (252) 995-4477
Hwy. 12, Hatteras Village
                         (252) 986-2900

Outer Beaches Realty offers around 600 homes throughout the seven villages of Hatteras Island. Properties are located on the sound, the ocean and everywhere in between. Some homes accommodate large parties.

Sun Realty

Hwy. 12, Salvo
(252) 987-2766   (800) 345-0910
Hwy. 12, Avon
(252) 995-5865   (800) 843-2034

One of the largest vacation rental companies on the northern Outer Banks, Sun Realty also covers Hatteras Island. They offer around 300 homes in all seven villages on the island, from the ocean to the sound and in between. Choose from condominiums to homes, from modest to luxury.

Surf or Sound Realty

Hwy. 12, Salvo   (252) 987-1444
Hwy. 12, Avon
(252) 995-5801   (800) 237-1138

Surf or Sound represents more than 400 homes in the seven villages of Hatteras Island. They specialize in premier and luxury homes, mostly for families and large groups. Homes range from four to 10 bedrooms. Homes are on the ocean, sound and in between.

Pet Accommodations

Hatteras Island Pet Resorts

Hwy. 12, Rodanthe   (252) 987-1127
Hwy. 12, Frisco   (252) 995-4851

The Hatteras Island Pet Resorts allow you to bring your pets on vacation, even if they aren't allowed at your own accommodations. Daily pickup and visitation are encouraged. Dogs can get private runs or share a run if they're from the same family. Cats and other animals are also accepted. Current immunization records are mandatory.

Sidenotes ❧

Hurricane Isabel

Photo courtesy: Hatteras Designs, Inc.

Cabanash Pond with houses.

The view looking north on Hwy. 12 leaving the village.

Photo courtesy: Hatteras Designs, Inc.

On Friday, September 19, 2003, after a full day's pounding from Hurricane Isabel the day before, the residents of Hatteras Island — those who decided to ride out the storm on the island — ventured out to survey the damage from the category 2 storm. Sand covered N.C. Highway 12 in many areas of the island. The oceanfront dunes were wiped flat in others. Wooden stairs and debris littered the beach as far as the eye could see. The island's three oceanfront piers had suffered damage. Roof shingles, chunks of house siding, tree limbs and debris peppered the villages. Great pools of salt water stood where they never had before.

But nothing could have come as more of a shock

than what the residents of Hatteras Village saw on the east end of their village. While most of Hatteras Village survived the storm unscathed, homes and buildings that were standing two days earlier on the east end were completely gone. Buildings were gutted or washed off their foundations. A motel straddled N.C. 12. The historic 1898 Durant Life-Saving Station had vanished. A house was floating in the Pamlico Sound. Stoves, refrigerators, air conditioners, furniture, personal belongings, splintered wood and rubble were scattered about the area. But the greatest shock was the vast river of water flowing from the ocean to the sound, across the area where N.C. 12 once connected Hatteras Village to Frisco. Three breaches formed the first new inlet on the island since 1962, cutting Hatteras Village off into its own island that would come to be known as "Little Hatteras."

Appliances and other goods ruined by the saltwater are piled along Hwy. 12.

Photo courtesy: Hatteras Designs, Inc.

The breach being filled.

Photo courtesy: Hatteras Designs, Inc.

See **www.hatterasguide.com** for full content, links & updates.

Sidenotes

(Below)A NOAA aerial showing the north end of Hatteras Village before Hurricane Isabel.

There were harrowing tales of the villagers who had endured the storm: a couple who spent hours in a tree, watching their home float away; a woman snatching her dog by the tail just before it floated off in the rushing water; a dramatic rescue on a surfboard; people sitting on their porches watching buildings float by; a sink hole swallowing buildings. Miraculously, no one was hurt or seriously injured on the entire island.

The people of Hatteras Village were devastated, but it didn't take long

for them to pull together. Relief personnel streamed into Hatteras Village – the National Guard, the Salvation Army, the Red Cross and volunteers from far and wide. The Salvation Army served meals in the Community Center, the county established a shelter at the Volunteer Fire Department, nondenominational church services were held for everybody, and portable showers were set up in the middle of the village. Those who were affected the least helped those who were affected the

Sidenotes ❧

The same view after Hurricane Isabel shows the destruction of the Durant Stion, General Mitchell and Sea Gull motels and a number of properties on the west side of what was once Hwy. 12 .

Photo courtesy: NOAA

Sidenotes ❧

Children returning from school on the school boat.

The dredge Illinois *pumped sand from Hatteras Inlet several miles south to fill in the breach.*

most. Supplies were boated in from all over the county, and volunteers from Frisco and other island villages came over daily. As time went by, power and water were restored, and cleanup and restoration began in earnest. Demolition crews and heaps of rubble were a constant sight on the east end. Children went back to school in Buxton, ferried over on the *Miss Hatteras* from Oden's Dock to Frisco Cove Marina and then transported by bus to the school. People went back to work.

The response to the Outer Banks'

newest inlet was quick. The U.S. Army
Corps of Engineers filled the inlet with
material dredged from the Hatteras
Inlet ferry channel, and the North
Carolina Department of Transportation repaired the 2,400-foot section of
road in six days. The highway was
reopened on November 18, 2003,
exactly two months after the inlet was
created. The road officially opened to
the public on November 22, once
again allowing people to access
Hatteras Village and Ocracoke via the
Hatteras Inlet Ferry.

Hatteras Village is back to normal.
The major cleanup has been done, and
the few homes and businesses that
were damaged are concentrating on
rebuilding or relocating. The village,
and the rest of the island, have made it
through another hurricane, just as
generations of islanders have done
before them. 🦎

Sidenotes ⚘

*What was once Hwy. 12 became an
inlet and then became Hwy. 12 once*

Photo courtesy: Hatteras Designs, Inc.

See **www.hatterasguide.com** for full content, links & updates.